Psychoanalytic Liberation Psychology

Psychoanalytic Liberation Psychology challenges conventional psychological paradigms by developing a radical approach where psychoanalysis meets liberation psychology.

Drawing from his psycho-political work in South Africa, Nick Malherbe articulates how this approach functions as a powerful counterforce to capitalism's psychological grip on society and individuals. Rather than presenting a definitive framework, this book offers theoretical insights alongside concrete case reflections that illuminate both the generative potential and inherent challenges of this work. Malherbe invites readers to participate in an ongoing dialogue about what psychoanalytic liberation psychology could become.

Psychoanalytic Liberation Psychology creates space for critical discourse about the role of both psychoanalysis and liberation psychology in anti-capitalist social movements. It will be essential reading for psychoanalysts, psychologists, and scholars across disciplines and will provide valuable insights for academics in psychoanalytic studies and psycho-political fields, while remaining accessible to practitioners seeking to integrate liberatory approaches into their work.

Nick Malherbe is a researcher at Institute for Social and Health Sciences, University of South Africa & South African Medical Research Council-University of South Africa Violence, Injury and Social Asymmetries Research Unit.

Psychoanalytic Liberation Psychology

Anti-Capitalist Approaches

Nick Malherbe

R Routledge
Taylor & Francis Group

LONDON AND NEW YORK

Designed cover image: Illana Welman. Kind thanks to Illana Welman for permission to use the image featured on the cover of this book: https://lanispice.co/.

First published 2026
by Routledge
4 Park Square, Milton Park, Abingdon, Oxon OX14 4RN

and by Routledge
605 Third Avenue, New York, NY 10158

Routledge is an imprint of the Taylor & Francis Group, an informa business

British Library Cataloguing in Publication Data
A catalogue record for this book is available from the British Library

Library of Congress Cataloging-in-Publication Data
A catalog record has been requested for this book

ISBN: 9781041010272 (hbk)
ISBN: 9781041010265 (pbk)
ISBN: 9781003612728 (ebk)

DOI: 10.4324/9781003612728

Typeset in Times New Roman
by Taylor & Francis Books

Contents

Acknowledgments

Building collective resistance to capitalism is a psychological undertaking as much as it is a political one. In struggle with others we pass through a range of desires, disappointments, fears, jubilations, and anxieties. Alongside our comrades we mourn, love, hate, rage, despair, and feel. However, that political struggles are always also sites of struggling psychologies does not mean that psychology and psychoanalysis should necessarily form part of our struggles. Indeed, neither of these two disciplines seem especially interested in turning away from capitalism's necropolitical regimes of expropriation and exploitation. Practitioners from both psychology and psychoanalysis have explicitly endorsed and tacitly complied with genocide and occupation in Palestine, apartheid in South Africa, torture throughout Latin America, US drone warfare, European austerity, deportations in the United States, land dispossession in Oceania – the list goes on and on. To put psychology and psychoanalysis to the work of anti-capitalism is, therefore, to enter an immensely contradictory space.

Over the last few years, I have learned from, been inspired by, worked alongside, and engaged with several people in South Africa who are, in different ways, undertaking what I understand to be anti-capitalist psychopolitical work: Sipho Dlamini, Peace Kiguwa, Garth Stevens, Ursula Lau, Ronelle Carolissen, Brett Bowman, Brendon Barnes, Fatima Seedat, Alex Freeman, Rashid Ahmed, Refiloe Makama, Debbie Kaminer, Kopano Ratele, Umesh Bawa, Mandisa Malinga, Sarah Day, Floretta Boonzaier, Haile Matutu, and Tumi Mpofu. There are also colleagues and comrades around the world who are undertaking this sort of work from whom I have learned a great deal: Christopher Sonn, Lara Sheehi, Urmitapa Dutta, Glenn Adams, Geetha Reddy, Ian Parker, Artemis Christinaki, Josephine Cornell, Rebecca Helman, Stephen Sheehi, Jesica Siham Fernández, James Ferreira Moura Jr., Monica Eviandaru Madyaningrum, Nadera Shalhoub-Kevorkian, and Devin Atallah, to name only some.

I could not have wished for a greater education in refusing, breaking away from, and reconstituting psychological praxis than that which has been given to me by my colleagues at the University of South Africa's Institute for

Social and Health Sciences (ISHS): Ghouwa Ismail, Naiema Taliep, Ashley van Niekerk, Lu-Anne Swart, Seneca James, Tshifhiwa Mokobedi, Simone Harris, Noxolo Dumani, Tiffany Hector, Jade Morkel, Nomagugu Ngwenya, Pascal Richardson, Munene Nkuna, Xolisa Gwadiso, Relebogile Rasodi, Anthony Phaahlamohlake, Jeanette Maritz, Jeminah Binase, Najuwa Arendse, Ncamisile Mbambo, Tumi Mashaba, Adelaide Sebothoma, and Sizwe Masango, among many, many others.

My thanks especially to ISHS colleagues Hugo ka Canham, whose break from the psy-disciplines has informed my cautious embrace of them; Daniel Radebe and Bongani Mavundla, both of whom I worked alongside during many of the reflections that appear in this book; as well as Shahnaaz Suffla and Mohamed Seedat, whose political education and caring mentorship have made possible navigating the rather woeful intuitions of academia.

I am indebted to the community members, social movements, and organisations in the south of Johannesburg with whom I have worked during my time at the ISHS.

My sincere thanks to Susannah Frearson and Saloni Singhania at Routledge for their kind and efficient assistance in getting this book published. And, indeed, to Ian Parker, for introducing me to Susannah.

Kind thanks to Illana Welman for permission to use the image featured on the cover of this book: https://lanispice.co.

Lastly, to Sam, whose commitment to love never seems to be deterred by an increasingly loveless global order.

Some of the chapters in this book are slightly modified versions of previously published material. Chapter 2 is drawn from my 2024 article "Fantasy and Anti-Capitalist Resistance: Some Implications for Psychoanalytic Liberation Psychology" published in the *International Journal of Applied Psychoanalytic Studies*, 21(4), e1894, reproduced here with permission; Chapter 3 is drawn from my 2024 article "Against the Superegoic Community: Community Psychology, Psychoanalysis, and the Consolidation of Political Communities" published by the *Annual Review of Critical Psychology*, 18, 1204–1222, reproduced here with permission; and Chapter 4 is drawn from my 2023 article "Unconsciousness-Raising: Considerations for Liberation Psychology, Subjectivity, and Reflexivity Theory", published in *Psychoanalytic Dialogues*, 33(4), 456–474, reproduced here with permission.

Chapter 1

Against Psychoanalysis, Against Psychology

Introduction

> Psychology as it is generally practiced is not geared to cure. Often it does not reach the root of the problem because it does not recognize the social origin of many forms of mental illness. How could the woman [in the prison cell] next door to me even begin to be cured if the psychologist treating her was not aware of the way in which racism, like an ancient plague, infects every joint, muscle and tissue of social life in this country? This woman was rotting in a snake pit of racism, flagellating herself daily with her obscene and graphic imagination. In order to understand her illness, it would be necessary to start with the illness of the society – for it was from the society that she had so perfectly learned how to hate Black people.
>
> – Angela Y. Davis (2022, p. 37)

> And a therapy that has proven worse than useless may eventually be replaced with the only thing that can do any good: political organization.
>
> – Shulamith Firestone (1970, p. 71)

In this book, I am concerned with how something called psychoanalytic liberation psychology might be put to work for anti-capitalist resistance. This concern, as we will see, is marked by several intractable contradictions. Indeed, we are putting two largely incompatible disciplines – psychology and psychoanalysis – into the service of an emancipatory agenda (anti-capitalism) to which both disciplines have, historically, been largely opposed. And while it should not be denied that contradictions like these can immobilise us and prevent us from acting, I will argue that they can also enliven us to the ever-shifting requirements of anti-capitalist struggle. As we will see, its internal contradictions mean that psychoanalytic liberation psychology is never quite settled or at one with itself. It is continually formed and reformed by the political and psychological composition of the anti-capitalist collective. If psychoanalytic liberation psychology practice seeks to give expression to emancipatory desire, it is also moulded by such desire.

DOI: 10.4324/9781003612728-1

Let us begin, then, by delving a little more deeply into the disciplinary and political contradictions that animate psychoanalytic liberation psychology. We will start with its disciplinary contradictions, which are undoubtedly familiar to those of us who have attempted to hold psychology together with psychoanalysis. Although there are certainly some – often 'repressed' – similarities that exist between psychology and psychoanalysis (Burman, 2016), they are not the same thing. Broadly speaking, we can mark the difference between psychology and psychoanalysis by their respective approaches to knowledge. Where most of psychology seeks to know the human subject through demarcated psychological components (e.g. personality, behaviour, cognition, health, biology; Roberts, 2015), psychoanalysis is by and large concerned with the unknowable, non-self-identical nature of subjectivity, which is to say, the unconscious desires that undermine the consciously 'known' subject (Stavrakakis, 2007). As Foucault (1965, p. 198) put it, psychoanalysis addresses itself to the human "experience of unreason that it has been psychology's meaning, in the modern world, to mask". Psychologists thus tend to distinguish themselves from psychoanalysts by insisting on the scientific nature of their discipline (Parker, 2007).

Of course, neither psychology nor psychoanalysis is homogeneous, and there are always exceptions to these kinds of generalising characterisations. It is often the case that psychologists and psychoanalysts adopt one another's techniques, terms, and approaches, blurring the line between the two (Colman, 2016). Indeed, Freud referred to some aspects of his pioneering work in psychoanalysis as psychology. Even Lacanian psychoanalysis, which tends to be bitingly critical of psychology, owes something of a "reluctant debt" to several psychological theories (Hook, 2017, p. 4). Nonetheless, to paint in necessarily broad strokes, if most of psychology strives to resolve the tensions that mark subjectivity, most psychoanalysis pivots on the assumption that tension is inherent to subjectivity and therefore cannot be done away with (Parker, 2014). Attempting to hold psychology with psychoanalysis often means ignoring these disciplinary contradictions by subordinating one (typically psychoanalysis) to the dictates of the other (usually psychology).

The second contradiction that we run into when articulating psychoanalytic liberation psychology is a political one. Although there have always been psychologists and psychoanalysts who are also committed activists in and outside of their practice, it remains the case that most of those working in the psy-disciplines have little to do with anti-capitalist politics. Psychologists and psychoanalysts tend to be reluctant to even name capitalism, despite income inequality, poverty, and individualised class-based competition being correlated with depression, low self-worth, and neuroses (see Bettache, 2024; Dev & Kim, 2020). It is far more often the case that psychology and psychoanalysis are drawn on to bolster the ideological mandate of capitalism (see Parker & Pavón-Cuéllar, 2021). Where mainstream psychology has been wielded to adjust subjects to the oppressive and exploitative dictates of capitalism (Roberts, 2015), mainstream psychoanalysis has been used to move subjects towards accepting their discontent – their "ordinary unhappiness" (Freud, 1955, p. 305) – under capitalism. The knowable, marketable, fixed, and controllable subjectivities that many psychologists and psychoanalysts interpellate in their clinical practice map well onto capitalist social arrangements (Morris, 2022). 'Good' subjectivity for much psychology and psychoanalysis has been confined to the nuclear family, with identity categories like gender and race essentialised or brushed aside in an apparent bid for clinical neutrality (Ghannam, 2005; Stevens, 2020; Weisstein, 1993). We have seen both psychology and psychoanalysis operating as instruments of discipline that turn structural oppression into problems of the individual, often via patriarchal, colonial, and elitist readings that pathologise political dissidence of any sort (Christinaki & Sheehi, 2023). All over the world, psychology and psychoanalysis have formed part of brutally violent statecraft, including racist apartheid labour policy, torture in Guantanamo Bay, US drone warfare, settler colonialism in Palestine and Algeria, and British colonial settlement in India (Eidelson, 2023; Fanon, 2018; Hartnack, 1987; Parker 2014; Seedat, 1997; Sheehi & Sheehi, 2022).

Given all of this, one might reasonably ask whether psychology or psychoanalysis have a place in anti-capitalist politics. Psychology and psychoanalysis may be too closely knit into the ideological infrastructure of capital accumulation to convincingly offer anything to anti-capitalist resistance. Even if we concede that organising anti-capitalism is a psychological undertaking – one that involves intergroup tension, trauma, and affective investments – it seems clear that neither psychology nor psychoanalysis are the only ways by which to pronounce on or understand the psychological processes underwriting anti-capitalism. The consciousness-raising of radical feminist and Black Consciousness groups, socialist conceptions of alienation, Indigenous and decolonial emphases on the entanglements of knowledge and being, and the anarchist practice of mutual aid all represent anti-capitalist approaches to the psychological which make little, if any, use of psychology and psychoanalysis.

It would appear, then, that if psychology and psychoanalysis are by and large opposed at the disciplinary level, they are united in a reactionary political orientation, one that aligns well with capitalist ideology. And while it cannot be denied that both disciplines have revealed important insights into our psychic functioning, neither has a monopoly on how we understand the psychological – especially how the psychological operates in relation to anti-capitalism. In light of all of this, to practise something called psychoanalytic liberation psychology would appear to be a self-defeating task. And yet, there is a politically dissident tradition of evoking psychology with and through psychoanalysis for purposes of anti-capitalist consolidation. It is a tradition that, following others (e.g. Hollander, 2023), I am calling psychoanalytic liberation psychology.

Psychoanalytic liberation psychology, I want to argue in this book, does not ignore the capitalist collusions that we observe in most of psychology and psychoanalysis. Rather, psychoanalytic liberation psychology takes up the contradictory task of striking back against the very capitalist order in which psychology and psychoanalysis were forged. To practise psychoanalytic liberation psychology is to recognise that we cannot ignore the psychological facets of emancipatory politics, nor can we collapse emancipatory politics into psychological categories. As Jameson (1986, p. 76) writes:

> When a psychic structure is objectively determined by economic and political relationships, it cannot be dealt with by means of purely psychological therapies; yet it equally cannot be dealt with by means of purely objective transformations of the economic and political situation itself, since the habits remain and exercise a baleful and crippling residual effect.

Recognising the complex, intractable entanglements of politics and psychology serves as the fundamental means by which psychoanalytic liberation psychology moves through its contradictory formation.

This book has two broad aims. The first is to develop a conceptual understanding of psychoanalytic liberation psychology. Here, I am less concerned with preserving psychoanalytic or psychological concepts in their original formulations than I am with (re)purposing these concepts to serve anti-capitalism. The book's second aim is to flesh out what psychoanalytic liberation psychology might look like in practice. As such, throughout the book, I offer illustrations and reflections from my own psychoanalytic liberation psychology work in South Africa (more on this later). In pursuing these two aims, I do not claim to provide a comprehensive or definitive outline of the theory and practice of psychoanalytic liberation psychology. Nor do I offer a global or regional history of psychoanalytic liberation psychology. Instead, through a context-specific set of theoretical, concrete, and reflective offerings, I hope that the book illuminates some of the challenges and generative potentialities of using psychoanalytic liberation psychology to engage the psycho-political dimensions of anti-capitalist resistance.

In the following sections, I provide a brief definition of anti-capitalism, the political orientation that guides my formulation of psychoanalytic liberation psychology throughout this book. I then describe how, against the capitalist collusions of mainstream psychology and psychoanalysis, some of the ways by which liberation psychology and psychoanalysis have been put to work for anti-capitalism. Lastly, I consider how anti-capitalism has been taken up by those practising a combination of liberation psychology and psychoanalysis (i.e. psychoanalytic liberation psychology) after which I outline each of the chapters that follow on from this one.

Anti-Capitalism

The term *anti-capitalism* seems to have entered into common parlance as recently as 1999, during the protests against the World Trade Organization Ministerial Conference that took place in Seattle that year. The range of resistance tactics and strategies employed by the protesters, as well as the different struggles that came together in the protests (e.g. environmentalism, labour, health, fair trade) were described, among other things, as anti-capitalist (Chatterton, 2010). The diversity of the political actions and struggles in Seattle was, however, offset by the lack of diversity among the protesters themselves. Protesters, and especially the protest leaders, tended to be white men from elite social backgrounds (Prempeh, 2004). The myopias of Seattle should not, however, be mistaken for the myopias of anti-capitalism.

Amin (1991, p. 85), writing a few years before the Seattle protests, reflected:

> [Capitalism] has brought to the forefront of the historical stage not 'socialist' revolutions led by the working classes of the developed capitalist countries but 'anti-capitalist' revolutions provoked by the polarization inherent in worldwide capitalist expansion, with socially intolerable consequences for the peoples of the peripheries and semi-peripheries of the system.

At the very same time as the Seattle protests, farmers and campesinos were waging hugely diverse mass struggles across Mexico (Solnit, 2016). These struggles were explicitly anti-imperialist and, indeed, explicitly anti-capitalist. It was also around the time of the Seattle protests that Argentina's National Front Against Poverty was mobilising trade unions, human rights organisations, and social movements (Campos, 2015). And two months before Seattle, South Africa saw one of the largest strike actions in the country's history, with six hundred thousand public workers downing their tools (Barchiesi, 1999). Observing the global revolutionary energies of this time, Bond (2014, pp. 161–162) writes that:

> Virtually all countries provided evidence, by the turn of the century, of coalitions and networks of anti-globalisation activists, many of which were fairly well grounded in mass democratic organisations that acted locally, but thought globally: for example (here we cite only a few simply to give a flavour of this current), Mexico's Zapatistas, Brazil's Movement of the Landless, India's National Alliance of People's Movements, Thailand's Forum of the Poor, the Korean Confederation of Trade Unions, Burkina Faso's National Federation of Peasant Organisations, the Canadian Halifax Initiative, the US '50 Years is Enough' campaign against the Bretton Woods institutions, and so on.

As long as there has been capitalism, there has been anti-capitalist resistance (Holloway, 2019). Anti-capitalism was never confined to Seattle, nor the year 1999.

Anti-capitalism is a negative term, defined by what it is not, by what it refuses. Thus, to understand anti-capitalism, we must first understand capitalism. Certainly, we owe much of what we know about capitalism to anti-capitalists. As Anderson (2025, p. 24) explains it, capitalism "rarely if ever spoke its own name in the nineteenth and for most of the twentieth century – the very term was an invention of its opponents". So, what is capitalism? Capital refers quite simply to the money that we use to make more money. Money, Marx (1973, p. 459) tells us, is one of the "antediluvian conditions of capital". Investments, factories, bonds, stocks, and land are all examples of capital. The stability of capitalism depends on the infinite growth of capital, on the ever-expanding quantities of nature and human labour that are pulled into circuits of accumulation (Hickel, 2020). If capital is not growing – expanding into new frontiers – then capitalism tends to fall into crisis. To meet these unrelenting growth demands, a capitalist economy relies on ever-increasing rates of exploited labour and rent extraction, as well as finance markets and debt peonage.

Capitalism is, however, more than just a growth economy. It is, Fraser (2022) argues, an institutionalised social order. This is to say that capitalist economic growth depends on under-compensated and uncompensated care work (like cooking, raising children, and cleaning), environmental destruction (including dumping, mineral extraction, and pollution,), neocolonialism (such as land enclosers, hyper-extractive trade relations between the Global North and South, and the destruction of Indigenous ways of being and knowing), and the oligarchic control of public institutions (noted in the rise of far-right and fascistic governments the world over, as well as increasingly high rates of austerity). Put differently, exploitative economic relations, the feminisation of reproductive care work, ecocidal domination, the statist control of civic life, and the degradation of racialised colonies and former colonies constitute the complex unity of capital (see Hall, 2021; Marx, 1973). We see, then, how capital accumulation fixes, destroys, stultifies, and separates identity, land, modes of (re)production, and how we relate to one another and the world around us. In short, the capitalist social order is imbibed by what hooks (2000, p. 46) calls "imperialist white supremacist capitalist patriarchy".

If capitalism is not just economy, but a broader social order (of which the economy is a central, but not the only, component), then anti-capitalist resistance demands not only a labour movement that refuses the exploitation of wage-earning workers, but also a range of other movements that refuse the degradation of care work; the destruction of the environment; colonial occupation, enclosures, and genocides; and the hollowing out of public institutions. These seemingly disparate fronts of struggle connect when we understand them as pushing back against the patriarchal, ecocidal, imperial, and racist forces of capitalism. The frictions within and between struggles can bind us to the multiple lines of attack that overthrowing capital's multifarious structures requires. If we are subordinate to the demands of capitalism, we are also insubordinate in the many ways by which we refute capital's dehumanising mandate. It is perhaps not useful, then, to look to anti-capitalism to provide a positive identification for the different struggles that fall within its orbit. As Holloway (2019, p. 13) puts it, "Dignity's revolt mocks classification". Instead, every struggle against capitalism is always already included in the significatory field of anti-capitalism (Malherbe, 2024). Anti-capitalism, we might say, operates as a generative counterattack within which visions of liberation bolster and consolidate one another (Simpson, 2017).

We see anti-capitalism in workplaces, educational institutions, places of worship, and in the home. We also see it in state institutions, the streets, and across borders. Anti-capitalists gather in person, online, the ancestral realm, and via the kinds of wisdom and legacies passed down in books, myth, political lineage, and tradition. Anti-capitalism moves with (and, necessarily, against) capitalism. It is, as Marx and Engels (1978, p. 163) wrote, "the real movement which abolishes the present state of things. The conditions of this movement result from the premises now in existence". At different moments and for different purposes, anti-capitalism might take on vertical, horizontal, collective, individual, communitarian, or non-hierarchical formations (Nunes, 2021). Moving through such different formations, geographies, actions, persons, and locations, anti-capitalism is never complete or foreclosed. We do not definitively arrive at anti-capitalism. We keep building it and thus we keep desiring it – approaching it without ever settling on a final or complete form (Malherbe, 2024). Anti-capitalism is always being written and rewritten to include more and more people who refuse capitalism's systematic degradation of land, labour, and life. In Bloch's (1975, p. 171) words, anti-capitalism represents a "processus cum figures, figurae in processu", an ongoing process that is made by those who are made by this process. Anti-capitalism moves between the wholesale rejection of the existing social order, limiting the capacities of this order, and building power from within it, thereby doing away with false distinctions between revolution and reform. Anti-capitalists seek to make the greatest possible change within and to capitalism, strengthening "the structural impact that our limited capacities to act can have" (Nunes, 2021, p. 290), while always looking beyond capitalism.

Anti-capitalism, it should be said, is not non-capitalism. Where non-capitalism exits capitalism (or at least tries to) without direct confrontation, anti-capitalism takes capitalism on. Community gardens, the solidarity economy, radical communes, care initiatives, and mutual aid efforts all represent non-capitalist formations. Non-capitalism can be drawn on by capitalist powers to shift the responsibility for the social wreckage wrought by capital onto poor and working people. The gulf between non-capitalism and anti-capitalism is not, however, unbridgeable. Non-capitalism can assume an anti-capitalist orientation when it operates alongside organised resistance efforts that confront capital. Non-capitalist community gardens become part of anti-capitalist resistance when they are linked to movements for food sovereignty, for example. On the flipside, non-capitalism can ensure that anti-capitalism is made ordinary; part of how we survive and live together in a social order premised on the negation of life. Non-capitalism, in other words, can make anti-capitalism part of the everyday. As Holloway (2019, p. 166) writes:

> If capital's struggle is to alienate, fetishise, and degrade humanity (the creativity that makes people human) into subordinate labour, then anti-capitalist struggle is simply the struggle against dehumanisation and for humanity, dignity, in other words, the everyday stuff of life.

Although the future we are moving towards will be non-capitalist, our fight must be anti-capitalist, with all non-capitalist fragments put into the service of this fight.

Anti-capitalism is not immune to co-optation. Recognising that capitalism causes harm to most people, those in power repeatedly seek to accrue popular appeal by speaking to this harm without addressing its capitalogenic roots. Trump, Netanyahu, Le Pen, Erdoğan, Modi, Meloni, and Bolsonaro have all, in different ways, advanced neo-fascist agendas by tapping into widespread dissatisfactions with capitalism, blaming disenfranchised populations for these dissatisfactions. Klein (2024) notes that in recent years, terms like *othering, moral panic, eco-fascism*, and *the deep state* – all of which were developed by anti-capitalists – have been successfully mobilised by prominent right-wing ideologues. For their part, liberal pundits have often expressed sympathies with anti-capitalist rhetoric while always stopping short of pairing these expressions with concrete proposals, such as returning dispossessed land to Indigenous populations (Simpson, 2017). Distinguishing liberal and reactionary strategies of co-optation is, however, not always easy to do. We have seen how the Democratic Party in the US and the Labour Party in Britain have supported imperialist intervention all over the world, including a genocide in Palestine, while simultaneously staking a claim to liberal egalitarianism. Part of the task of building anti-capitalism is, then, to refuse its co-optation.

For some, the broadness of struggles signified by anti-capitalism detracts from the term's political use-value. Anti-capitalism, so the argument goes, signifies too much and thus cannot offer a durable political programme, concrete political principles, or a consistent set of strategies and tactics to which people can commit (see Malherbe, 2024). Recalling the 2001 Mayday demonstrations in London, Callinicos (2003, p. 106) writes that "a group of cyclists carried a banner proclaiming 'GET RID OF CAPITALISM AND REPLACE IT WITH SOMETHING NICER!' The slogan was intended

ironically, in order to draw attention to the vagueness of anti-capitalists."
Although there is certainly merit to arguments like these, I hope to have
made clear that the scale of capitalism and the existential urgency to dismantle it renders anti-capitalism a necessarily audacious means by which to
understand, organise, and forge connections between a multitude of different
struggles – bringing these struggles into a commonly articulated, always-in-
process project of emancipation. Contra accusations of vagueness, the
particularities of anti-capitalism are located across the different struggles that
comprise it, with each particularity morphing through the process of anti-
capitalist articulation. Anti-capitalism offers visions and experiences of a
world outside of capitalism in its millions of experiments in resistance and
living otherwise.

The formation of anti-capitalism is far from simple, and those who make
anti-capitalism do not always use this term. Yet, as Hickel (2020, p. 25)
argues, "While most people may not describe themselves as anti-capitalist,
survey results nonetheless show that large majorities question core tenets of
capitalist economics". Moving from questioning to challenging capitalism,
however, necessitates the intensely agonistic psycho-political work of articulating different struggles into a common formation. And while there are
undoubtedly many ways by which we might undertake this work, I will look
at how we might do so through a combination of psychology and psychoanalysis. As we have already seen, owing to the close ideological alignment
that psychology and psychoanalysis have with capitalism, this is not a simple
task. But it is also not an impossible one. In what follows, I examine some of
the ways by which psychology and psychoanalysis have, respectively, been
taken up by capitalist and anti-capitalist forces, after which I consider how
anti-capitalists might hold together both disciplines to form psychoanalytic
liberation psychology.

Psychoanalysis, Capitalism, Anti-Capitalism

Psychoanalysis has never represented a singular or coherent tradition. It
comprises many – often incompatible – approaches, methods, theories, and
practices (Colman, 2016). Although psychoanalysis was formalised by Sigmund Freud in the late nineteenth and early twentieth century, much of what
has come to be thought of as psychoanalytic practice existed well before
Freud. With all of this in mind, we can understand psychoanalysis in its
broadest sense as a therapeutic practice and system of thinking. Offering an
alternative to medical psychiatric approaches to distress, psychoanalysts
listen carefully to their clients, or rather, their analysands. Through this deep
listening, psychoanalysts work with analysands to make connections between
the analysand's past experiences and their present state of being (Parker &
Pavón-Cuéllar, 2021). Typically, the analysand will not have made these
connections prior to the analysis. This is because doing so requires a

confrontation and reckoning with past traumas which have been repressed; made unconscious. It is because we cannot consciously accept a particular experience that we make it unconscious. Although that which has been made unconscious has a determining or motivating influence on our thoughts, actions, and emotions, the unconscious is not accessible through ordinary introspection (Freud, 2005). The unconscious represents a kind of unknown knowledge, and its functioning (rather than its content) is revealed in the other side of our language, which is to say, the slips, dreams, symptoms, mistakes, mis-hearings, miscommunications, and repetitions that do not necessarily make coherent sense, even to ourselves. Psychoanalysis posits that exploring and reflecting on the repressed, unconscious elements of our psyche, and grappling with the kinds of misrecognition and conflict that we experience, can lead to insights that compel people to make changes in their lives (Lear, 2005).

Although psychoanalysis began as a treatment for neurotic illnesses, towards the end of his life, Freud came to think of psychoanalysis in a more general way, applying it as a system of thought for explaining human behaviour and society (Bettelheim, 1982). Our desires, anxieties, and drives, he argued, afford us insight into society precisely because these psychological phenomena are socially organised. In this regard, psychoanalysis denotes a broad-based investigation into how the world outside of us (history, culture, society, political economy) structures the psyche; what is inside of us.

These two conceptions of psychoanalysis – a mode of therapy and a sociological system of thinking – are not unrelated. Just as all psychoanalytic thinking takes its origins from therapeutic practice, psychoanalysis as a therapy is motivated by sociological psychoanalytic thought. As Jacoby (1977, p. 122) puts it, "Psychoanalysis is a theory of an unfree society that necessitates psychoanalysis as a therapy". We cannot entirely disavow psychoanalytic therapeutic practice, even when it is psychoanalytic social theory that we are using, and vice versa.

What, then, of psychoanalysis and capitalism? More often than not, psychoanalysis has served as an ideological tool for adapting subjects to the demands of capitalism – identifying psychic contradictions and tensions only to cover these up with the fantasies of subjective wholeness offered by the ideological promises of capitalism, such as upward mobility, commodities, power, and security (Rada, 2022). A psychoanalysis of this sort is willed towards acquiescence, pushing analysands to accept things as they are, with disappointment elevated to the status of virtue (Parker, 2011). When psychoanalysis hems so closely to the capitalist status quo, free association (i.e. sharing thoughts without the requirement of coherence in an attempt to access unconscious processes) tends to regress into meaningless chatter, with the psychoanalyst playing the role of a sympathetic listener who repeats what analysands say without interpretation, ignoring all tensions and digressions (Jacoby, 1977; Parker, 2011). In this, psychoanalysis becomes an exercise in bourgeois decadence (Timpanaro, 2011); a marketable, costly, time-consuming, and pragmatic therapy for self-improvement under capitalism, one that pivots on accepting capitalism (see Gherovici, 2018).

How we practise or use psychoanalysis under colonial capitalism raises several questions which Freud did not consider adequately. Reflecting on her work with poor and working-class Puerto Rican analysands living in the US, Gherovici (2013, p. 4) writes that much psychoanalysis has tended to operate under the assumption that "the poor cannot afford to have an unconscious". In post-1994 South Africa, Lau (2021) argues that, for many Black South Africans, the ongoing, stark, and structural nature of racialised violence can leave little room for repression. During the twentieth century's US-backed dictatorships in Argentina, Uruguay, and Chile, Hollander (2018) found that free association was hindered precisely because free expression of any sort was extremely dangerous during this time. Sheehi and Sheehi (2022) have noted that in occupied Palestine, psychoanalytic practice is quite literally interrupted by settler violence. They recount an instance of when teargas fired by Israeli soldiers onto Palestinians entered into a consulting room in Bethlehem. Although these sorts of oppressive social conditions are fundamental to people's psychic lives, most psychoanalysts turn away from them, preferring instead to take shelter in the analysand's denials, sources of infantile anxiety, or the transference relationship (Hollander, 2018).

In many respects, capital's imperial mandate forms part of psychoanalysis's epistemological infrastructure. Freud's conception of psychoanalysis undoubtedly rests on several racist assumptions that are rooted in colonial ideology (see, for example, his 'speculative anthropology'; Freud, 1913), and some of the language he used directly reflected this ideology, including "primal horde", "primitive man", and "cannibalistic savage" (Manganyi, 2018). For much psychoanalysis, colonised subjects have been presented as lacking, backwards, and/or perverse (Sheehi & Sheehi, 2024). Psychoanalysis was central to consolidating the colonial ideologies of the British Raj (Hartnack, 1987); advancing Eurocentric epistemic erasure in South Africa (Crewe, 2001); and supporting US-backed authoritarianism in Latin America (Hollander, 2023). Today, psychoanalysis has been taken up to prepare Israeli soldiers for torturing Palestinian prisoners (Hawa, 2024), and to consolidate settler colonial outposts (Sheehi, 2024). Indeed, if psychoanalysis bears the stamp of colonialism, it has also been part of coloniality's contemporary operations.

There are many other instances of psychoanalysis being utilised to advance the ideological mandate of capital accumulation. In the 1950s, for example, Jaques (2013 [1951]) used psychoanalysis to weaken trade union negotiations in the UK and to dismiss worker claims of persecutory management. It was also around this time that Edward Bernays – Freud's nephew – took up his uncle's work to establish what we now refer to as public relations. Bernays's work was instrumental in the propaganda campaigns that supported US imperialism in Latin America (Ewen, 1996). Some have drawn on psycho-analytic ideas to argue that the poor desire their poverty unconsciously, or that culturally sanctioned responses to capitalist oppression serve as legit-imate grounds for pathologisation (Gherovici, 2013). There are psycho-analytic practitioners who have used the discipline to police people's sovereignty and assist the liberal capitalist state in controlling, managing, and denigrating particular psyches, bodies and subjects in accordance with colonial logic – delineating who is deserving of rights and empathy, and who is perverse, deviant, and thus undeserving of the right to a dignified life (Sheehi & Sheehi, 2024).

Mitchell's (1973, p. xiii) well-known dictum that "psychoanalysis is not a recommendation for a patriarchal society, but an analysis of one" certainly holds up in many respects. However, it also seems clear that misogyny and androcentrism are baked into the practice, language, institutions, training, supervision, assumptions, and concepts of much psychoanalysis. Freudian-influenced theories on gendered personality differences have, for example, been drawn on to justify patriarchal subordination (Kessi et al., 2021). Psy-choanalytic concepts like the Oedipal Complex have been taken up by a number of psychoanalysts to naturalise heteronormativity (Parker & Pavón-Cuéllar, 2021). There appears to be an impulse among many psychoanalysts to control sexual and gendered organisation and expressions, especially among transgender analysands (Saketopoulou & Pellegrin, 2023; Wark, 2022). Chamberlain (2022) notes that psychoanalysts almost instinctively blame the analysand's mother for any and all distress in their lives, and that gendered oppression is usually ignored in the consulting room, with femin-ism either castigated or passed over in silence. There are recorded instances of women being sexually violated by their analysts (Carter, 2024). Queer people have also been humiliated, made deviant, subjected to 'conversion', or silenced within and by psychoanalysis (see Carter, 2024; Wark, 2022). Even self-proclaimed progressive psychoanalytic thinkers have succumbed to psy-choanalysis' patriarchal impulses. Much Freudo-Marxism, for instance, advocates for a kind of libidinal self-gratification (Parker & Pavón-Cuéllar, 2021), or an asocial morality in relation to the pleasure principle (Rustin, 1982), both of which hold the realisation of individualistic hedonism within the structures of capitalism – rather than anti-capitalist feminist liberation – as their ultimate goal.

Carter (2025) reveals how psychoanalytic institutions have, over the years, colluded with the oppressive dictates of colonial capital. He notes that many of today's psychoanalytic institutions are organised around cults of person-ality that are geared towards accruing cultural and financial capital by investing in and imposing the standards of whiteness, heteronormativity, imperialism, and racism, with any sort of liberatory agenda almost com-pletely absent within these intuitions (see also Sheehi & Sheehi, 2022). Indeed, as Sheehi and Sheehi (2024) highlight, the International

Psychoanalytic Association, the International Association for Relational Psychoanalysts and Psychotherapy, and the New Lacanian Society have all held conferences in Israel's apartheid settler colony. They note that many of those embedded in these psychoanalytic institutions claim to know the psychology of a fundamentally traumatised Other, and with this knowledge attempt to exert a patronising, violent kind of colonial control.

Psychoanalysis has, historically, had a rather hostile view of anti-capitalism; trivialising, individualising, and dismissing political dissidence as a product of neurosis (Cooper, 2013), and relegating the material basis of class antagonism to unconscious processes of psychic splitting or projection (Parker, 2007; Timpanaro, 2011). Freud, for his part, tended to offer regressive or, by his own admission, inadequate political analyses that depoliticised the most urgent material issues of his day (Dolar, 2009). He tended to see revolutionary ideas as illusory consolations, arguing in some of his writing that psychoanalysts should stay clear of politics altogether (Tomšič, 2015). Freud's supposed analytic neutrality remains cherished by many psychoanalysts who have refused to engage with, let alone act or speak out against, oppressive social systems (Rada, 2022). We saw this in the apparent 'neutrality' of psychoanalysts practising in brutally violent regimes, such as fascist Germany, apartheid South Africa, and South America's US-backed dictatorships (see Hollander, 2023). And we see it in the pseudo-neutrality – or what Sheehi and Sheehi (2022) call psychoanalytic innocence – adopted by the psychoanalysts who refuse to say or do anything about Zionist-led occupation and genocide in Palestine.

In light of all of this, it is certainly possible to argue – as, indeed, some have argued (e.g. Collier, 1980) – that because most psychoanalysis has allied with the violent mechanisms of capital accumulation, while also corroding anti-capitalist resistance, all that psychoanalysis can offer to anti-capitalists is a means by which to manage their neuroses so that they might commit more effectively to advancing anti-capitalist struggle. Yet, the task of dismantling oppressive capitalist structures and institutions is always also a task of dismantling the ways by which these structures and institutions exploit, disturb, and even excite the human psyche. Resisting capitalism involves considerable repression, unconscious desire, trauma, pleasure, transference, and pain – all of which are central to psychoanalysis. And while most psychoanalysis has acted to reproduce colonial capitalist social relations, there also exists a tradition of putting psychoanalysis to the work of undoing these relations (Sheehi & Sheehi, 2024); of consolidating anti-capitalism by paying attention to the internal distortions, contradictions, and displacements that mark anti-capitalist movements (see Leland, 1988; Tomšič, 2015).

Freud, as we know, did not align himself with anti-capitalism, and there is a notable social and cultural conservatism that stains much of his writing (Dolar, 2009). Curiously, though, he worked alongside several political radicals. Wilhelm Reich, Alfred Adler, Otto Fenichel, and many other disciples of

Freud were all committed to an avowed anti-capitalist politics. Indeed, the Berlin Psychoanalytic Institute was, during Freud's time, a place where socialists were attempting to articulate a Marxist approach to practising psychoanalysis (Fuechtner, 2011). Later, the free Sexpol Clinics set up by Reich sought to understand sexual repression under capitalism (Robinson, 1969).

There are moments in Freud's work (albeit not many) where one could be forgiven for mistaking him for a political radical, such as when he writes "It goes without saying that a civilization which leaves so large a number of its participants unsatisfied and drives them into revolt neither has nor deserves the prospect of a lasting existence" (Freud, 1927, p. 12). Freud believed that psychoanalysis served as an important means of probing into the kinds of alienation and psychic oppression taking place in the industrial capitalism of his time (Parker & Pavón-Cuéllar, 2021). Perhaps most radically, he insisted that poor and working-class people should have access to psychoanalytic therapy, and in 1920, he established the first free clinic, the Berlin Poliklinik (Danto, 2005). Other free clinics were eventually set up across Europe and North America. Later, clinicians all over the world would take inspiration from Freud's free clinic initiative, working to ensure that psychoanalysis is not only free, but that it takes seriously the kinds of racism, sexism, and state violence to which historically marginalised communities are subjected under capitalism (Gherovici, 2018). For example, both the Women's Therapy Centre in London (founded in 1976) and the Women's Therapy Centre Institute in New York (founded in the early 1980s) blended psychoanalysis and radical feminism (Hollander, 2023). The moments of anti-capitalism within Freudian psychoanalysis and its legacy require our careful and dialectical assessment. In conversation with her sister, Taiwo Afuape reflects that "The more I learnt about Freud the more I came to see him as both an upholder of oppressive values and a staunch critic of them" (Afuape & Afuape, 2015, p. 203). We do well to hold this dual conception of Freudian psychoanalysis in mind when we consider what psychoanalysis might mean for anti-capitalism.

If we accept that capitalism cannot ever hail us completely into its orders of meaning, and that freedom and resistance can be located in those moments which defy such orders of meaning (Hollander, 2023), then psychoanalysis can serve as a resource for political praxis (Stavrakakis, 2007), taking anti-capitalist politics away from notions of mastery, management, and unchallenged conviction (Parker, 2011), and towards the immanent points of tension and incoherence revealed by the unconscious. Psychoanalysis, it should be emphasised, cannot reveal the objective mechanisms of our social worlds. And although we should not seek political salvation in psychoanalysis, it can play a role in consolidating anti-capitalist struggle by revealing the kinds of conflicts and dissociations underlying this struggle (Parker & Pavón-Cuéllar, 2021). Psychoanalysis can be used to illuminate psychic mechanisms of repression, thereby encircling reality's points of contradiction so that we can take up a political position relative to these contradictions (Ingleby, 1984). It is with psychoanalysis that we are able to gain a deeper understanding of how our desires can undermine the demands that society or even our anti-capitalist political commitments place on us as individuals. Psychoanalysis can enable us to probe into the capitalist forces which simultaneously foster oppression and liberatory fantasy (Gherovici, 2018). To connect psychic and structural processes in these ways has the potential to move people to institute subjective changes which correspond to the changes they wish to make in society (Parker, 2011).

Psychoanalysis's anti-capitalist tradition is not singular. A wide range of psychoanalytic approaches have been taken up by anti-capitalists, including Freudian (e.g. Jeffries, 2016), Kleinian (e.g. Rustin, 1982), Fanonian (e.g. Maldonado-Torres et al., 2021), Lacanian (e.g. Pavón-Cuéllar & González Equihua, 2013), Bionian (e.g. Sheehi & Sheehi, 2023), and Winnicottian (Gerard, 2023). There is also considerable literature drawing on psychoanalytic theory that offers important criticism of the imperial, ecocidal, gendered, racialised, authoritarian, exploitative, and colonial elements of capitalism (e.g. Fanon, 2018; Hollander, 2018; Memmi, 2013; More, 2021; Parker, 2011; Popa, 2018; Rada, 2022; Saketopoulou & Pellegrin, 2023; Stavrakakis, 2007; Stevens, 2020; Tomšič, 2015; Valdés, 2022). Moreover, there have been many efforts to bring together psychoanalytic practice and anti-capitalist resistance, as noted in the communist and anti-fascist movements in post-war France (Althusser, 2014; Guattari, 1977); clinical practitioners in Algeria (Fanon, 2018) and Palestine committed to decolonisation (Sheehi & Sheehi, 2022); radical community practitioners in South Africa (Maldonado-Torres et al., 2021); feminist and queer activists throughout Europe (Valdés, 2022; Leland, 1988; Mitchell, 1973; Popa, 2018); post-Marxists in Latin America (Cavooris, 2017); socialist and post-anarchist movements the world over (Parker & Pavón-Cuéllar, 2021; Rousselle & Evren, 2011); decolonial and Marxist psychoanalytic practitioners in Cuba (Lacerda, 2015); dialectical materialist psychoanalytic practitioners in the Soviet Union (Hristeva & Bennett, 2018); Africana existentialists (More, 2021); left-wing movements collaborating with public health organisations in Argentina (Hollander, 2023); anti-capitalist militants in Brazil (Tupinambá, 2021); and anti-authoritarians throughout Latin America (Hollander, 2023). In each of these cases, the theories and concepts of psychoanalysis are or were taken up by those directly confronting the imperial mechanisms of capital accumulation.

Psychoanalysis, it should be underlined, does not offer us an anti-capitalist political programme of any sort. Carter (2024) insists that although we should not displace the anger that we rightly hold towards psychoanalysis, we can use this anger as an invitation to repair psychoanalysis and take responsibility for its history of oppression; its collusion with colonial capital.

As Mitchell (1973) notes, it is not necessarily what Freud and his followers did that is important for our struggles today, but rather how we can use their work politically. Instead of taking up psychoanalysis exactly as Freud did, anti-capitalists can repeat the gesture of Freud's thinking with an awareness of its limits, looking instead to the emancipatory traditions that have taken place in and alongside psychoanalysis (Tupinambá, 2021). This is the fundamentally contradictory position in which anti-capitalist psychoanalysts find themselves. It is a position that is similarly occupied by the anti-capitalist psychologist.

Psychology and Capitalism; Liberation Psychology and Anti-Capitalism

At the broadest level, psychology can be understood as "the science of the nature, functions, and phenomena of behaviour and mental experience" (Colman, 2016, p. 4). This definition assumes that all behaviour and psychic activity is determined by laws that are rational and, therefore, observable. There is, however, something unsatisfactory about hitching psychology to a single definition. Depending on where in psychology one stands, its definition seems to change. Cognitive psychologists, behavioural psychologists, developmental psychologists, and social psychologists all emphasise some aspects of psychology, while downplaying or disavowing others. Parker (2007) argues that instead of trying to grasp psychology with specific, often competing, definitions, we should look to the nineteenth-century industrial capitalist societies of Europe. Indeed, it was in these societies, shaped by empire and white supremacism, that a privatised, atomised, colonial, and competitive conception of success began to emerge (Holdstock, 2000; Kessi et al., 2021). And it was in – and, crucially, for – these societies that a set of variable practices known as psychology was formally developed (see Danziger, 1990).

The whiteness, Eurocentrism, heteronormativity, and "world-colonising" (Ratele, 2019, p. 14) epistemic frames that mark psychology have been well-documented (see e.g. Guthrie, 2004). In many respects, psychology emerged out of the same colonial episteme as psychoanalysis (Manganyi, 2018) – managing, adapting, defining, adjusting, individualising, pathologising, and rendering docile subjects in accordance with the dictates of colonial capital (Pavón-Cuéllar, 2017; Seedat & Suffla, 2017). Yet, psychology has also colluded with capitalism in ways that differ somewhat from psychoanalysis. Where an argument can be made that in the early formulations of psychoanalysis, Freud and his contemporaries were concerned with critically interrogating the kinds of alienation and neuroses that were taking place in the nuclear family under capitalism, this was not the case for psychology (Parker, 2014). Psychology was always intended to work with and for capital. Bassiri (2024) demonstrates how nineteenth-century psychological practitioners assessed people's well-being in accordance with their economic performance as well as imperial standards of white masculinity. With its proclivity towards managing and measuring worker preference, psychology would eventually find fertile ground in the personnel departments of European factories (Parker, 2007), the legacy of which can be observed in contemporary practices of industrial/organisational psychology (Merhej & Makarem, 2025). Psychologists were also key contributors to scientific racism (see Kessi et al., 2021), obsessing over the intelligence, brain size, morals, criminality, and sexuality of Black subjects (Winston, 2020). This fundamentally racist episteme remains operational in some strands of contemporary psychological research (Hendricks et al., 2019; Howitt & Owusu-Bempah, 1994; Ratele, 2019).

Much psychological practice is guided by what Moghaddam (2010) calls the embryonic fallacy, whereby the self-contained, sovereign individual is taken as the source and centre of all psychological experience. Through the embryonic fallacy, the structure of the world is interpreted through an individual's psychological functioning – bodies and brains; attitudes and beliefs (Roberts, 2015). This is why many of the treatments proposed by psychology, such as cognitive behavioural therapy, pivot on short-term, highly individualised adaptation and atomisation (Merhej & Makarem, 2025). Psychology's individualisation of the subject abstracts the self from context, alienating people from their experience while enforcing an entrepreneurial understanding of the self as a kind of development project; with growth, competitiveness, affect management, and self-regulation positioned as crucial to one's sense of fulfilment and wellbeing (Adams et al., 2019). By over-representing these traits, psychology acts to universalise them, naturalising subjectivity as fundamentally capitalistic (Bettache, 2024). Accordingly, psychology's 'good' subjects take responsibility for their wellbeing by contributing to or minimally disrupting the accumulation of capital, whereas its 'bad' – apparently maladjusted – subjects do not, cannot, or refuse capital's subjective hail (see Parker, 2007).

For mainstream psychology, the political is always, at its core, psychological. Intergroup racist hostility is, for example, projected by much psychology as an inevitable and unchangeable, if perhaps also unfortunate, facet of human nature (Holdstock, 2000). Alternatively, psychology might tell us that oppressive proclivities are not a part of human nature, but a case of human nature gone wrong. Fascism is simply an issue of maladjusted personalities (Bettache, 2024), and climate change can be traced to individual behaviour and feelings (Oladejo et al., 2024). The individual is the beginning and end of politics for psychology, and is thus the point at which all change-making must focus. As such, the best we can hope for, mainstream psychology tells us, is for political tensions (including political oppression) to be neutralised in the image of liberal tolerance (Parker, 2007). Individual actions rather than collective struggle are always, in this respect, centralised. Consequently, the structure of the capitalist social order – along with how race, gender, coloniality, and ecological destruction coalesce under this order – recedes from psychology's purview.

We can see, then, how most of today's psychological knowledges, products, and practices are put into the service of legitimising, bolstering, and reproducing the individualising authority of capitalist ideology (Adams et al., 2019). If, as Hall (2021, p. 22) writes, "the capitalist mode of production depends on social connection assuming the 'ideological' form of an individual disconnection", then psychology has served to consolidate this ideological disconnection by attributing an individual's social position to an asocial conception of their agency, work ethic, and ingenuity (Schabas, 2007). Despite this, many psychologists are invested in the status of psychology as a non-ideological science. For these psychologists, it is only psychology's detractors who are ideological and/or unscientific (Augoustinos, 1999; Merhej & Makarem, 2025). Accordingly, much of psychology is preoccupied with the concepts and concerns of the natural sciences, confining the psychological to that which can be measured and observed (preferably through experimentation), and excluding that which might be considered 'irrational', including the unconscious (Hook, 2017). Indeed, that psychology is a humanist science tends to be repressed; papered over by an insistence on the discipline's status as a natural science that deals strictly in universals (many of which are derived from psychological research that relies on the white male as a prototype for 'normality' and 'civilisation'; Kessi et al., 2021). Psychologists cling to the idea of psychology as a non-ideological science precisely because if the discipline is understood as operating from a place of pure scientific hubris (see Dlamini, 2024), then it can lay claim to the Enlightenment mandate, confidently making pronouncements on everything, everywhere (Malherbe et al., 2021). In this, the psychologist as a biased, partial subject becomes invisible.

There are many examples of psychology appealing to scientism in an attempt to legitimise itself and veil its ideological collusions with capitalism. Much of the discipline, for instance, employs a kind of factual rhetoric – often through orthodox experimental methods (Tissaw & Osbeck, 2007) – whose success depends on how it speaks to and reformulates dominant capitalist ideology (Billig, 1991). Psychology has also long presented something of an obsession with racist and sexist modes of measurement which naturalise social hierarchies (Laher, 2024). This was patently clear, Cooper (2014) has shown, in South Africa's history of psychological testing. Psychology's desperation to be taken seriously as a science is perhaps no more apparent, though, than in the Diagnostic and Statistical Manual of Mental Disorders (DSM), whose categories of psychological well-being are, in many cases, arbitrary and culturally biased. Indeed, the interpretive frameworks developed by Francis Galton, the founder of eugenics, were readily taken up in the DSM (Chapman, 2023). Many of the 'disorders' in the DSM are determined by a vote rather than empirical evidence, and it was only through activist pressure that 'homosexuality' was removed from the DSM in 1973 (Cooper, 2004). In all of these ways, we see how psychology appeals to scientism so that it can claim to *know* the subject (see Adams et al., 2019), thus aligning with a mechanism of colonial capitalist control that Mamdani (2012) refers to as *define and rule*.

Psychology's epistemological enterprise is defined largely by an etic approach, whereby its theories and methods, despite being derived mostly from Western European and North American contexts, are applied universally (Laher, 2024). As a result, many psychologists in the Global South feel a kind of pressure to conduct their practice in ways that are recognisable to the discipline's Eurocentric frames (Merhej & Makarem, 2025). The US, for example, dominates psychology's journals, teaching curricula, and institutions (Bettache, 2024). Much of psychology is conducted in English – and, to a lesser degree, Western European languages – to the exclusion of the languages and lifeworlds of the majority of the world's population in the Global South (Dlamini, 2024). That which falls outside of psychology's etic frame tends to be individualised and exoticised. Africa, for instance, is taken to be a site of fixed cultural difference, wherein material anti-colonial questions over land and dignity are displaced for an abstracted focus on memory and cognition (Ratele et al., 2020). We also see this in places like Palestine, where 'mental health NGOs' appear unable to break from individualistic and Eurocentric approaches to psychological practice (Makkawi, 2009); in Australia, where psychology's racism has shown to have a potentially negative impact on forensic outcomes among Indigenous populations (Gillies, 2013); and in apartheid South Africa, where psychology's first institution, established just two months after the National Party government came to power, was geared towards committing psychologists to white supremacist ideologies in their knowledge-making, teaching, and clinical practices (Cooper, 2014). Indeed, all over the world, psychology routinely ignores, dismisses, attacks, erases, or fetishises Indigenous knowledges (Adams et al., 2019), amounting to a kind of epistemological violence (Malherbe et al., 2021).

Psychology has, time and time again, shown itself to be invested in heteronormativity. It has been complicit in enforcing gendered binarism and stereotypes, policing gender expression through pathologisation and medicalisation (Kessi et al., 2021). Much of psychology appears unable to read queerness, just as it seems unable to read blackness, within its epistemological registers (Merhej & Makarem, 2025). Yet again, when psychology does endeavour to understand racial or gendered oppression, it tends to do so through an individualising lens, focusing on prejudice and discrimination as they manifest in attitudes and personality, thereby ignoring agency and resistance to the racist and sexist structures upon which capital accumulation depends (Kessi et al., 2021). Accordingly, ka Canham (2024) emphatically states that psychology's investment in whiteness, cis-heteronormativity, and Eurocentrism has meant that it has failed Black, queer, and Indigenous life.

Most psychologists tend not to question the rigid hierarchies of capital upon which their interpretive systems are based. All over the world, we see psychology's complicity with capitalist oppression, whether this be in liberal capitalist democracies (Malherbe, 2023), Israel's apartheid regime (Makkawi, 2009), or the fascist orders of Italy and Germany (Hollander, 2023; Volpato, 2000). Such complicity often takes the form of silence; a retreat into the apparent political neutrality of scientism. However, psychology's complicity has also been more directly observable, as seen in psychologists' involvement in refining torture techniques and normalising drone warfare (Eidelson, 2023), or the part that white South African psychologists played in the apartheid state's military, police force, prisons, secret police, and intelligence services (Cooper, 2014).

Psychology, it would then seem, is a thoroughly capitalist discipline. If, as Kruger (2024, n.p.) writes, "Psychologists do not know what to do with hungry people", it also does not know what to do with anyone who lies outside of capital's white, cis-heteronormative, Euro-American centric bourgeois class structures (Kessi et al., 2021). Psychology, as we have come to know it, functions as a commodity to be bought, advertised, supplied, speculated on, and sold in the market, with little space made for socio-political justice (Merhej & Makarem, 2025). Indeed, positivist rigour seems to be cherished over any sort of societal relevance (Dutta, 2018). And yet, psychology is not singular. There have always been attempts – marginal as they may be – to develop psychology otherwise (Decolonial Psychology Editorial Collective, 2021); to commit the discipline to a broadly anti-capitalist agenda. Many times, practising psychology otherwise relates to naming and seeking to understand capitalist oppression through the languages and frameworks of those at the sharpest end of this oppression (Bettache, 2024). In other words, we see psychology otherwise in those attempts to situate the discipline on a new paradigm, one that is oriented towards emancipatory political practice. This is a psychology not of individualising management, discipline, and adaptation, but of liberation. It is what Martín-Baró (1994) and others (see e.g. Caparros & Caparros, 1976) called *psicología de la liberación*; or, liberation psychology.

To speak of liberation psychology is not to speak of a particular approach to practising psychology, or even to a specific kind of psychology, but rather to a politically committed paradigm from within which to undertake psychological work (Burton & Guzzo, 2020). It is thus the psycho-social requirements of emancipation, as they are articulated by oppressed social classes, that determine liberation psychology (Malherbe, 2018). This means that liberation psychology is often embedded, guided by, and evoked within anti-capitalist social movements (Burton & Gómez, 2015).

When trying to understand what liberation psychology is, one might reasonably seek to find out when liberation psychology was first implemented. This is not a simple task. Pinpointing the moment at which psychological knowledges were first put into the service of consolidating anti-capitalist struggle is neither possible nor, I would argue, desirable. As already noted, those waging anti-capitalist struggle have always been in some way attentive to the psychological. Nonetheless, we can attribute the popularisation of liberation psychology as a named paradigm to the work of Martín-Baró (1994), a Spanish-born Jesuit priest and social psychologist working in El Salvador in the 1970s and 1980s (Burton & Guzzo, 2020). It was in response to the crisis of relevance that marked social psychology in the 1970s that Martín-Baró set out to do for psychology what several radical Latin American theologians were, at the time, doing in their religious practice, namely, establish a "preferential option for the poor" (Beers, 1985, p. 944). Martín-Baró was not alone in this. In the Philippines, Guatemala, Palestine, Venezuela, and South Africa, among others (Enriquez, 1992; Lykes, 1999; Makkawi, 1999; Montero, 1998; Seedat, 1997), liberation psychology practitioners insisted that oppression is maintained through capitalism's political, colonial, cultural, economic, and social structures, and that because psychic distress emerges out of these structures, a socially and politically relevant psychology must locate and address distress at the structural level. Thus, by rejecting the universalism and scientism of mainstream psychology, liberation psychology the world over sought to situate the psyche in society so that we might better work to change society (Montero et al., 2017; Seedat, 1997).

Martín-Baró (1994) outlined three suitably broad elements of liberation psychology: (1) a new horizon, where psychology moves away from attaining legitimacy and recognition from capitalist institutions, moving instead towards the needs of oppressed populations; (2) a new epistemology, where psychological knowledge is understood as a contextually embedded process that is shaped by collectives, rather than discovered or imposed by professionals; and 3) a new praxis, where people work together to develop a structural understanding of the world so that they might act to change the world based on these understandings. Martín-Baró (1994) was also fond of several pragmatic values that he insisted would advance these three elements of liberation psychology. These values included de-ideologising everyday reality, de-alienation, reorienting psychology, recovering historical memory, honouring peoples' virtues, conscientisation, problematisation, sensitivity towards power dynamics, praxis, and de-naturalisation (Rivera, 2020).

The liberation psychology label has not, in every instance, been taken up by those practising what we might think of as liberation psychology (Malherbe & Canham, 2024). And although liberation psychology does not denote a specific field of psychology, some psychological fields have taken to the liberation psychology paradigm more readily than others, such as social psychology, eco-psychology, educational psychology, cultural psychology, Indigenous psychology, and – especially – community psychology (see Montero et al., 2017). Similarly, even though liberation psychology is not reliant on a singular epistemological frame, much liberation psychology is grounded in participatory models that emphasise social action, dialogue, horizontal communication, and reflexivity (see e.g. Seedat et al., 2017; Watkins & Shulman, 2008). This does not, however, mean that statistically oriented methods and approaches have been expelled from liberation psychology praxis (see e. g. Dorling & Simpson, 1999). Certainly, Martín-Baró (1994) himself made extensive use of surveys and statistics. The point of liberation psychology is always to prioritise the demands of liberation over psychology, no matter the field or methodological orientation within which one's work is situated.

Over the years, liberation psychology practitioners have passed through and taken up many anti-capitalist traditions (see Comas-Díaz & Rivera, 2020), including, for instance, Marxism (Malherbe, 2018; Pavón-Cuéllar & González Equihua, 2013) and radical feminism (Domínguez, 2022; de Oliveira et al., 2009). There is, however, an especially strong tradition of decolonising liberation psychology work (some of which predates Martín-Baró), as noted, for instance, in the work of Fanon (1986 [1967]), Bulhan (1985), and Manganyi (2019 [1973]). In more recent years, the decolonial attitude has had a pronounced influence on liberation psychology praxis taking place in the Global South (see e.g. Bhatia, 2019; Boonzaier & van Niekerk, 2019; Carolissen & Duckett, 2018; Kessi et al., 2022; Seedat & Suffla, 2017). Here, liberation psychology has been put into the service of addressing border violence, land reform, disability justice, genocidal violence, solidarity-building, securing housing, and a host of other urgent anti-capitalist struggles (see Sonn et al., 2024).

Martín-Baró did not believe that liberation psychology was able to supplant the necessarily political processes required to consolidate anti-capitalist resistance. And yet, as so many have argued, while anti-capitalism cannot be reduced to psychology, it also cannot ignore psychology. Martín-Baró (1994, p. 45) wrote that "It is not the calling of the psychologist to intervene in the socioeconomic mechanisms that cement the structures of injustice, it is within the psychologist's purview to intervene in the subjective processes that sustain those structures of injustice and make them viable". These interventions are never foreclosed. Liberation psychology is a paradigm that remains open to being transformed and led by the most politically urgent analyses and actions being carried out on the ground. It is a psychology produced in and for struggle, and it is therefore a psychology that is always in flux, morphing in accordance with the demands of struggle. It is for this reason that liberation psychology has never been shut off from other, seemingly incompatible, disciplines. Indeed, it has, on occasion, found fertile ground in the insights of psychoanalysis.

Psychoanalytic Liberation Psychology

As we have already noted, to bring psychoanalysis into the liberation psychology paradigm is to commit to a "clandestine alliance" (Morris, 2022, p.

5), one that is fraught with several disciplinary and political contradictions which are not always grappled with adequately (see Afuape, 2012). As such, a number of psychologists and psychoanalysts have expressed doubts regarding the emancipatory prospects of this clandestine alliance. Parker (2022) has argued that because most of those who work in the liberation psychology paradigm refuse to acknowledge the unconscious, liberation psychology has, in some cases, struggled to break decisively from psychology's individualising impulses to know the subject definitively (see also Moane, 2003). Liberation psychology's rootedness in psychology – critiquing it while also relying on its frameworks and epistemes – means that it risks inadvertently imposing a fixed grid on human subjectivity, whereas psychoanalysis, in its more progressive iterations, cannot but read subjectivity in and against broader social relations (Mitchell, 1971). On the flipside, many liberation psychology practitioners remain unconvinced by the emancipatory capacities of psychoanalysis. Although Martín-Baró (1994) was influenced by several psychoanalytic thinkers, such as Erich Fromm, Wilhelm Reich, Frantz Fanon, and Sigmund Freud, he believed that psychoanalysts had, by and large, served the same project of capitalist management and adaptation that mainstream psychology had. And indeed, scholars like Barratt (2011) have drawn on Martín-Baró's insights to critique psychoanalysis in this manner.

While the incompatibilities of psychoanalysis and liberation psychology should not be ignored, it is also possible, I am arguing, that bringing both together can hold each accountable to the demands of anti-capitalism in dynamic ways. As Parker (2014, p. 41) writes, we can use psychoanalysis to "help us to work in and against the discipline of psychology, and in and against psychoanalysis to stop it turning itself into another form of psychology, and to bring it closer to critical psychology". By practising psychoanalytic liberation psychology in and through a plurality of formations, we refuse the reactionary impulses that mark psychology and psychoanalysis, subjecting both to the kinds of social change that anti-capitalists seek to implement in all economic, political, and cultural institutions (Tupinambá, 2021).

How, then, can we practise psychoanalytic liberation psychology through its contradictions? Fundamentally, liberation psychology takes psychoanalysis into the community contexts from which psychoanalysts, qua psychoanalysts, tend to refrain. On the other side, psychoanalysis takes liberation psychology in directions it might otherwise approach with trepidation, if at all. It is through psychoanalysis that liberation psychology is urged to ask what enjoyment and sacrifice mean for emancipatory politics; how knowledge might obstruct solidary building; in what ways political oppression effects psychic repression; how the past lives in the present through repetition; in what ways temporality influences the building of grassroots power; and how individual subjectivity is hailed by the anti-capitalist collective. Psychoanalysis's interruption of the knowable, the secure, and the good can, therefore, guard against liberation psychology practitioners unconsciously falling into psychology's determinist mould (e.g. by stabilising representation or obscuring internal tension).

Freud (1965, p. 158) asserted that psychoanalysis does not offer to us a *Weltanschauung,* which is to say, psychoanalysis is not a worldview that "solves all the problems of our existence uniformly on the basis of one over-riding hypothesis, which, accordingly, leaves no question unanswered and in which everything that interests us finds its fixed place". Liberation psychology is similarly bereft of a definitive worldview, encompassing instead a range of epistemic positions and political standpoints (Malherbe & Canham, 2024). Curiously enough, anti-capitalism *does* represent a worldview, one that is – to borrow from Graeber and Wengrow (2021) – *schismogenic*; constituted by what it is not. Yet, unlike most other worldviews, anti-capitalism is willed towards its own annihilation; towards creating equitable, non-capitalist social conditions that, by definition, do not require anti-capitalism. If, then, psychoanalytic liberation psychology praxis is shaped and guided by anti-capitalism's schismogenic worldview, it becomes clear that those undertaking such praxis need not invest in apprehending psychology or psychoanalysis 'correctly'. Indeed, we approach the forms, possibilities, and limits of psychoanalytic liberation psychology through the anti-capitalist struggles that take place outside of psychology and psychoanalysis (see Pavón-Cuéllar, 2017).

It is perhaps easier to proclaim what psychoanalytic liberation psychology is not, rather than what it definitively is. Indeed, psychoanalytic liberation psychology is not concerned with psychological interpretation divorced from action (Afuape & Afuape, 2015), nor with dressing up already existing concepts and practices in new theoretical garb – usually for purposes of developing and selling yet another specialised silo of applied psychoanalysis/psychology (Bruns & Barron, 2022). It is not even especially invested in itself. We should be willing to abandon any and all psychoanalytic liberation psychology practice that does not directly contribute to anti-capitalist struggle (see Afuape & Afuape, 2015). Anti-capitalist practitioners like Fanon (2018) were well aware that there will undoubtedly be moments when the sheer materiality of struggle has little use for psychological interpretation or Freudian insights into the symbolic. As he put it, the "rifle of the Senegalese soldier is not a penis but a genuine rifle, model Lebel 1916" (Fanon, 1986 [1967], p. 106).

There are, however, many examples that we can look to of how psychoanalytic liberation psychology has been practised. Psychoanalytic liberation psychology has, for example, been considered in relation to emancipatory struggles in South Africa (Barratt, 2011) and Russia (Kuppersmith, 2000), and there have been attempts to articulate psychoanalytic liberation through the work of specific thinkers, such as Jacques Lacan (Beshara, 2022; Pavón-

Cuéllar & González Equihua, 2013) and Frantz Fanon (Maldonado-Torres et al., 2021; Sheehi & Sheehi, 2022).

Psychoanalytic liberation psychology practice was part and parcel of the struggle against the 1970s and 1980s US-backed military dictatorships in South America. Anti-capitalist therapists working in these contexts during this time understood their work as "psychoanalysis in the tradition of liberation psychology" (Hollander, 2023, p. 429). In Argentina, for instance, psychoanalysts working in the Argentine Psychiatric Federation and the Organization of Mental Health Workers served as volunteers in public health projects initiated by left-wing political organisations operating in working-class neighbourhoods and settlements (Hollander, 2023). After the dictatorships fell, these same clinicians became involved in struggles against neoliberalism and neo-colonialism, insisting – as they always did – that social justice must form part of how we understand and approach psychological wellbeing (Hollander, 2023).

In their work, Sheehi and Sheehi (2022, p. 177) have engaged with "the robust community of clinicians throughout historic Palestine committed to psychoanalytically informed liberation psychology". Shalhoub-Kevorkian (2020) has drawn on psychoanalytic liberation psychology to understand how Palestinian children reflect on and contextualise their experiences of colonial violence. Further, Shalhoub-Kevorkian has, along with several others, used psychoanalytic liberation psychology to explore how women in Palestine struggle against the patriarchal violence enacted by Israeli settlers, paying particular attention to the role that feminist critical consciousness plays in this struggle (see Cavazzoni et al., 2023). Psychoanalytic liberation psychology has, in short, formed part of how Palestinians resist and survive Zionist occupation, imprisonment, torture, and genocide.

Building resistance to capitalism necessitates building collective power. Differently wounded psychological subjects are required to work together to build such power. They do so in fraught social conditions that are not of their making and that are always at risk of mirroring the oppressive capitalist order being struggled against. Psychoanalytic liberation psychology addresses itself to these junctures of struggle, finding form in psycho-political processes willed towards relating, acting, organising, living, and being in the sorts of radically egalitarian ways that have been disallowed by capitalism.

This Book

The biases and limitations folded into this book's prose emerge out of my historically embedded subjectivity, political commitments, and disciplinary background. I am white, male, cis-gendered, and able-bodied. I was born in South Africa at a time when the apartheid system was being formally dismantled and reconfigured into a racial capitalist order. That I have benefited in material ways from South Africa's colonial history is incontestable. That these benefits were built on upturning and destroying the lives of millions of Black South Africans is similarly incontestable.

In South Africa, under-resourced communities were engineered for Black populations under the colonial and, later, apartheid systems. Consequently, these communities came to represent reproductive sites of dual power, wherein social movements, workers, trade unions, political organisations, and laypeople collaborated to strike back at white supremacism and capital (Bond et al., 2013). From the mid-2000s, community-led social movements in South Africa's urban and rural areas have represented the strongest sites of anti-capitalist opposition in the country (see Duncan, 2016). Indeed, throughout South Africa, these community movements have advanced the sharpest attacks, analyses, and mitigations of racial capitalist violence (see Alexander, 2023; Bond, 2014; Kessi et al., 2022; Manganyi, 2019 [1973]). Over the years, my colleagues and I have worked with several community movements in the south of Johannesburg to develop a kind of psychoanalytic liberation psychology. While some psychoanalytic liberation psychology practitioners are trained psychoanalysts who work in the liberation psychology paradigm (see e.g. Hollander, 2023), I am a community psychologist (more of which is discussed in Chapter 3) whose liberation psychology praxis has been influenced by psychoanalytic theory. As I recount in more detail in Chapter 4, South Africa's long colonial history weighs heavily on this work.

Each of the following chapters focuses on a concept that I have found to be pertinent in the psychoanalytic liberation psychology practice with which I have been involved. These concepts include political fantasy, the superegoic community, unconsciousness-raising, memory otherwise, and the Not-Yet. I attempt to illustrate each of these concepts with a case reflection. These reflections are not to be read as psychological case formulations or psychoanalytic case presentations. As Parker (2018) has made clear, case presentations and case formulations offer truncated snapshots of what are, in reality, prolonged, intensive, and highly variable engagements. As such, case presentations and case formulations tend to collapse into a kind of voyeuristic gossip. Conversely, the case reflections offered in this book are expressly partial, incomplete, and – I hope – open to re-reading. None of the reflections that I recount claims to capture every feature of the particular concept that they seek to explore. On the contrary, they might be said to undermine these concepts by yoking them to a specific instant recalled by one person (Tupinambá, 2021).

In Chapter 2 I flesh out some of the progressive and regressive valences of political fantasy. I consider what fantasy means for capitalism, and what it means for practising psychoanalytic liberation psychology with communities undertaking anti-capitalist movement building. I then reflect on how psychoanalytic liberation psychology may and may not be of use to community activists whose political activity is undergirded by a bricolage of fantasies, breakdowns in fantasy, and attempts at holding reality accountable to emancipatory fantasies.

In Chapter 3 I draw from critical community psychology and Lacanian psychoanalysis to argue that the ethical task of psychoanalytic liberation psychology is not to eradicate the superego's influence on communities, but to minimise its influence by making clear its obscene and unremitting command to enjoy capitalism. This ethical task requires that psychoanalytic liberation psychology practitioners work with community activists to consolidate political communities, wherein enjoyment is structured by sacrifice and collectively constituted political goals. I then reflect on how South African social movement actors built a political community founded on anticapitalist solidarity to combat the xenophobia demanded by the superegoic community.

Both liberation psychology and psychoanalysis have, historically, been part of consciousness-raising groups. In Chapter 4 I consider how those working within psychoanalytic liberation psychology might foreground the unconscious in consciousness-raising processes (i.e. unconsciousness-raising). Departing from Fanon and Lacan, I argue that unconsciousness-raising has the potential to shift the activist subject's relationship to unconscious identifications in accordance with their consciously professed anti-capitalist commitments, and to harness the emancipatory potential of desire in relation to these commitments. Then, reflecting on my own work, I examine what the unconsciousness-raising process might mean for the collective constitution of political subjectivity, and how this process can trouble static conceptions of reflexivity theory.

In Chapter 5 I am concerned with memory. I argue that for psychoanalytic liberation psychology, the central aim of memory work is not to retrieve memory wholesale, but to engage memory otherwise, that is, to approach the past through the kinds of temporalities and affects that have been disallowed by capitalist time. I then turn to my own work, which engages the memory work taking place in Johannesburg South's land-based community struggles. More specifically, I look at how land activists bring the past to bear on the present by engaging with fragmented, sometimes incompatible, memories of community and community struggle.

In Chapter 6, the concluding chapter, I draw on Ernst Bloch's conception of the Not-Yet (as well as the notions of hope and utopia folded into the Not-Yet) to read and make connections between the four hitherto concepts explored in this book, namely: political fantasy, the superegoic community, unconsciousness-raising, and memory otherwise. I then consider what the Not-Yet means for anti-capitalist community movements in South Africa, movements which have guided the conception and practice of psychoanalytic liberation psychology that has been outlined in this book.

References

Adams, G., Estrada-Villalta, S., Sullivan, D., & Markus, H. R. (2019). The psychology of neoliberalism and the neoliberalism of psychology. *Journal of Social Issues*, 75(1), 189–216.

Afuape, T. (2012). *Power, resistance and liberation in therapy with survivors of trauma: To have our hearts broken*. Routledge.

Afuape, T., & Afuape, T. (2015). Is psychoanalysis a liberation approach? African sisters in dialogue. In T. Afuape & G. Hughes (eds), *Liberation practices: Towards emotional wellbeing through dialogue* (pp. 199–210). Routledge.

Alexander, N. (2023). *Against racial capitalism: Selected writings*. Pluto Press.

Althusser, L. (2014). *On the reproduction of capitalism: Ideology and ideological state apparatuses*. Verso.

Amin, S. (1991). The issue of democracy in the contemporary Third World. *Socialism and Democracy*, 7(1), 83–104.

Anderson, P. (2025). Idées-forces. *New Left Review*, 151(1). 19–34.

Augoustinos, M. (1999). Ideology, false consciousness and psychology. *Theory & Psychology*, 9(3), 295–312.

Barchiesi, F. (1999). The public sector strikes in South Africa. *Monthly Review*. Retrieved from https://monthlyreview.org/1999/10/01/the-public-sector-strikes-in-south-africa/.

Barratt, B. B. (2011). Ignacio Martín-Baró's "Writings for a Liberation Psychology" forum: Inspiring psychoanalytic writing. *Psycho-analytic Psychotherapy in South Africa*, 19(2), 121–134.

Bassiri, N. (2024). *Madness and enterprise: Psychiatry, economic reason, and the emergence of pathological value*. University of Chicago Press.

Beers, M. A. (1985). Preferential option for the poor: Liberation theology in Brazil. *New York University Journal of International Law and Politics*, 18, 921–967.

Beshara, R. (2022). A liberation psychoanalytic account of racism. *Awry: Journal of Critical Psychology*, 3(1), 77–94.

Bettache, K. (2024). Where is capitalism? Unmasking its hidden role in psychology. *Personality and Social Psychology Review*, 29(3). doi:10.1177/10888683241287570.

Bettelheim, B. (1982). *Freud and man's soul*. Alfred A Knopf.

Bhatia, S. (2019). Searching for justice in an unequal world: Reframing indigenous psychology as a cultural and political project. *Journal of Theoretical and Philosophical Psychology*, 39(2), 107–114.

Billig, M. (1991). *Ideology and opinions: Studies in rhetorical psychology*. Sage.

Bloch, E. (1975). *Experimentum mundi*. Suhrkamp.

Bond, P. (2014). *Elite transition: From apartheid to neoliberalism in South Africa*. Pluto Press.

Bond, P., Desai, A., & Ngwane, T. (2013). Uneven and combined marxism within South Africa's urban social movements. In C. Barker, L. Cox, J. Krinsky, & A. G. Nilsen (eds), *Marxism and social movements* (pp. 233–258). Haymarket Books.

Boonzaier, F. & van Niekerk, T. (eds). (2019). *Decolonial feminist community psychology*. Springer.

Bruns, G., & Barron, J. (2022). Psychoanalysis and the community–introductory considerations. *The International Journal of Psychoanalysis*, 103(1), 108–119.

Bulhan, H. A. (1985). *Frantz Fanon and the psychology of oppression*. Plenum Press.

Burman, E. (2016). *Deconstructing development psychology*, 3rd ed. Routledge.

Burton, M., & Gómez, L. (2015). Liberation psychology: Another kind of critical psychology. In I. Parker (ed.), *Handbook of critical psychology* (pp. 348–355). Routledge.

Burton, M., & Guzzo, R. (2020). Liberation psychology: Origins and development. In L. Comas-Díaz & E. T. Rivera (eds), *Liberation psychology: Theory, method, practice, and social justice* (pp. 17–40). American Psychological Association.

Callinicos, A. (2003). *Anti-capitalist manifesto*. Polity.

Campos, L. E. (2015). The National Front against poverty: The struggle for income redistribution. *Global Labour Journal*, 6(3), 351–365.

Caparros, A., & Caparros, N. (1976). *Psicología de la liberación*. Fundamentos.

Carolissen, R., & Duckett, P. (eds). (2018). Teaching toward decoloniality in community psychology and allied disciplines [Special issue]. *American Journal of Community Psychology*, 62.

Carter, C. J. (2024). On being angry with psychoanalysis forever. *Studies in Gender and Sexuality*, 25(1), 1–9.

Carter, C. J. (2025). American psychoanalytic institutes: Where academic freedom goes to die. *Psychoanalysis, Culture & Society*, 30(1), 113–131.

Cavazzoni, F., Veronese, G., Sousa, C., Ayoub, H., & Shalhoub-Kevorkian, N. (2023). Critical consciousness from a Palestinian feminist, decolonial perspective: A collective exploratory inquiry. *Feminism & Psychology*, 33(4), 451–470.

Cavooris, R. (2017). Intellectuals and political strategy: hegemony, posthegemony, and post-Marxist theory in Latin America. *Contemporary Politics*, 23(2), 231–249.

Chamberlain, M. (2022). *Misogyny in psychoanalysis*. Phoenix Publishing House.

Chapman, R. (2023). *Empire of normality: Neurodiversity and capitalism*. Pluto Press.

Chatterton, P. (2010). So what does it mean to be anti-capitalist? Conversations with activists from urban social centres. *Urban Studies*, 47(6), 1205–1224.

Christinaki, A., & Sheehi, L. (2023). The unconscious matters: Sexuality, violence, regimes: A short conversation with Lara Sheehi. *Studies in Gender and Sexuality*, 24(4), 219–225.

Collier, A. (1980). Lacan, psychoanalysis and the left, *International Socialism*, 2(7), 51–71.

Colman, A. (2016). *What is psychology?* Routledge.

Comas-Díaz, L., & Rivera, E. T. (eds). (2020). *Liberation psychology: Theory, method, practice, and social justice*. American Psychological Association.

Cooper, B. (2013). *A new generation of African writers: Migration, material culture & language*. Boydell & Brewer.

Cooper, R. (2004). What is wrong with the DSM?. *History of Psychiatry*, 15(1), 5–25.

Cooper, S. (2014). A synopsis of South African psychology from apartheid to democracy. *American Psychologist*, 68, 837–847.

Crewe, J. (2001). Black Hamlet: Psychoanalysis on trial in South Africa. *Poetics Today*, 22(2), 413–433.

Danto, E. A. (2005). *Freud's free clinics*. Columbia University Press.

Danziger, K. (1990). *Constructing the subject: Historical origins of psychological research*. Cambridge University Press.

Davis, A. Y. (2022). *Angela Davis: An autobiography*. Haymarket Books.

de Oliveira, J. M., Neves, S., Nogueira, C., & De Koning, M. (2009). Present but unnamed: feminist liberation psychology in Portugal. *Feminism & Psychology*, 19(3), 394–406.

Decolonial Psychology Editorial Collective. (2021). General psychology otherwise: A decolonial articulation. *Review of General Psychology*, 25(4), 339–353.

Dev, S., & Kim, D. (2020). State-level income inequality and county-level social capital in relation to individual-level depression in middle-aged adults: A lagged multilevel study. *International Journal of Environmental Research and Public Health*, 17(15), 5386.

Dlamini, S. (2024). *Beyond the pretty white affair: Training Africa-centring psychologists for the future*. Unisa Press.

Dolar, M. (2009). Freud and the political. *Theory & Event*, 12(3), 15–29.

Domínguez, D. (2022). Abolitionist feminism, liberation psychology, and Latinx migrant womxn. *Women & Therapy*, 45(2–3), 207–225.

Dorling, D., & Simpson, L. (eds). (1999). *Statistics in society: The arithmatic of politics*. Arnold.

Duncan, J. (2016). *Protest nation: The right to protest in South Africa*. University of KwaZulu-Natal Press.

Dutta, U. (2018). Decolonizing "community" in community psychology. *American Journal of Community Psychology*, 62(3–4), 272–282.

Eidelson, R. (2023). *Doing harm: How the world's largest psychological association lost its way in the war on terror*. McGill-Queen's University Press.

Enriquez, V. G. (1992). *From colonial to liberation psychology: The Philippine experience*. University of the Philippines Press.

Ewen, S. (1996). *PR! A social history of spin*. Basic Books.

Fanon, F. (1963). *The wretched of the earth*. Grove Press.

Fanon, F. (1986 [1967]). *Black skin, white masks*. Pluto.

Fanon, F. (2018). *Alienation and freedom*. Bloomsbury Publishing.

Firestone, S. (1970). *The dialectic of sex: The case for feminist revolution*. Bantam Books.

Foucault, M. (1965). *Madness and civilization: A history of insanity in the age of reason*. Tavistock.

Fraser, N. (2022). *Cannibal capitalism: How our system is devouring democracy, care, and the planet and what we can do about it*. Verso.

Freud, S. (1913). Totem and taboo. In J. Strachey (ed., trans.), *The standard edition of the complete psychological works of Sigmund Freud, vol. 13*. Hogarth Press.

Freud, S. (1927). The future of an illusion. In J. Strachey (ed., trans.), *The standard edition of the complete psychological works of Sigmund Freud, vol. 21*. Hogarth Press.

Freud, S. (1955). Studies on hysteria. In J. Strachey (ed., trans.), *The standard edition of the complete psychological works of Sigmund Freud, vol. 2*. Hogarth Press.

Freud, S. (1965). *New introductory lectures on psychoanalysis*. Norton.

Freud, S. (2005). *The unconscious*. Penguin.

Fuechtner, V. (2011). *Berlin psychoanalytic: Psychoanalysis and culture in Weimar Republic Germany and beyond*. University of California Press.

Gerard, N. (2023). *Winnicott and labor's eclipse of life: Work is where we start from*. Routledge.

Ghannam, J. (2005). The use of psychoanalytic constructs in the service of empire: Comment on Baruch (2003). *Psychoanalytic Psychology*, 22(1), 135–139.

Gherovici, P. (2013). Let's beat up the poor!. *CR: The New Centennial Review*, 13(3), 1–28.

Gherovici, P. (2018). Introduction. In P. Gherovici & C. Christian (eds), *Psychoanalysis in the barrios: Race, class, and the unconscious* (pp.1–18). Routledge.

Gillies, C. (2013). Establishing the United Nations' Declaration on the Rights of Indigenous Peoples as the minimum standard for all forensic practice with Australian indigenous peoples. *Australian Psychologist*, 48(1), 14–27.

Graeber, D., & Wengrow, D. (2021). *The dawn of everything: A new history of humanity*. Penguin.

Guattari, F. (1977). Everybody wants to be a fascist. *Semiotext(e)*, 2(3), 62–71.

Guthrie, R. V. (2004). *Even the rat was white: A historical view of psychology*. Pearson Education.

Hall, S. (2021). *Selected writings on Marxism*. Duke University Press.

Hartnack, C. (1987). British psychoanalysts in colonial India. In M. Ash & W. Woodward (eds), *Psychology in twentieth-century thought and society* (pp. 233–252). Cambridge University Press.

Hawa, K. (2024). Like a bag trying to empty: On the Palestinian prisoner and martyr Walid Daqqa. Retrieved from www.parapraxismagazine.com/articles/like-a-bag-trying-to-empty.

Hendricks, L., Kramer, S., & Ratele, K. (2019). Research shouldn't be a dirty thought, but race is a problematic construct. *South African Journal of Psychology*, 49(3), 308–311.

Hickel, J. (2020). *Less is more: How degrowth will save the world*. Random House.

Holdstock, T. L. (2000). *Re-examining psychology: Critical perspectives and African insights*. Routledge.

Hollander, N. (2018). Psychoanalysts bearing witness: Trauma and memory in Latin America. In P. Gherovici & C. Christian (eds), *Psychoanalysis in the barrios: Race, class, and the unconscious* (pp. 38–53). Routledge.

Hollander, N. C. (2023). *Uprooted minds: A social psychoanalysis for precarious times*. Routledge.

Holloway, J. (2019). *We are the crisis of capital: A John Holloway reader*. PM Press.

Hook, D. (2017). *Six moments in Lacan: Communication and identification in psychology and psychoanalysis*. Routledge.

hooks, b. (2000). *Feminism is for everybody*. Pluto Press.

Howitt, D., & Owusu-Bempah, J. (1994). *The racism of psychology: Time for change*. Harvester Wheatsheaf.

Hristeva, G., & Bennett, P. W. (2018). Wilhelm Reich in Soviet Russia: Psycho-analysis, Marxism, and the Stalinist reaction. *International Forum of Psychoanalysis*, 27(1), 54–69.

Ingleby, D. (1984). The ambivalence of psychoanalysis. *Free Associations*, 1, 39–71.

Jacoby, R. (1977). *Social amnesia: A critique of contemporary psychology*. Harvester.

Jameson, F. (1974). *Marxism and form: Twentieth-century dialectical theories of literature*. Princeton University Press.

Jameson, F. (1986). Third-World literature in the era of multinational capitalism. *Social Text*, 15, 65–88.

Jaques, E. (2013 [1951]). *The changing culture of a factory*. Routledge.

Jeffries, S. (2016). *Grand hotel abyss: The lives of the Frankfurt School*. Verso.

ka Canham, H. (2024). The black failure of psychology – an errant walking away. *Annual Review of Critical Psychology*, 18, 1298–1311.

Kessi, S., Boonzaier, F., & Gekeler, B. S. (2021). *Pan-Africanism and psychology in decolonial times*. Palgrave Macmillan.

Kessi, S., Suffla, S., & Seedat, M. (eds). (2022). *Decolonial enactments in community psychology.* Springer.

Klein, N. (2024). *Doppelganger: A trip into the mirror world.* Random House.

Kruger, L-M. (2024). Hunger. Retrieved from https://herri.org.za/10/lou-ma rie-kruger-hunger.

Kuppersmith, J. (2000). A liberation psychoanalysis for Russia. *American Imago,* 57 (1), 71–81.

Lacan, J. (2002). *Écrits.* Norton.

Lacerda, F. (2015). Insurgency, theoretical decolonization and social decolonization: Lessons from Cuban psychology. *Journal of Social and Political Psychology,* 3(1), 298–323.

Laher, S. (2024). Advancing an agenda for psychological assessment in South Africa. *South African Journal of Psychology,* 54(4), 515–530.

Lau, U. (2021). Between Fanon and Lacan: Rupturing spaces for the return of the oppressed. *Studies in Gender and Sexuality,* 22(4), 278–292.

Lear, J. (2005). *Freud.* Routledge.

Leland, D. (1988). Lacanian psychoanalysis and French feminism: Toward an adequate political psychology. *Hypatia,* 3(3), 81–103.

Lykes, M. B. (1999). Doing psychology at the periphery: Constructing just alternatives to war and peace. *Peace and Conflict,* 5(1), 27–36.

Makkawi, I. (1999). *Collective identity development among Arab-Palestinian students in Israel: Context, content, and process.* ERIC Clearinghouse.

Makkawi, I. (2009). Towards and emerging paradigm of critical community psychology in Palestine. *Journal of Critical Psychology, Counselling and Psychotherapy,* 9, 75–86.

Maldonado-Torres, N., France, M. F. M., Suffla, S., Seedat, M., & Ratele, K. (2021). Fanon's decolonial transcendence of psychoanalysis. *Studies in Gender and Sexuality,* 22(4), 243–255.

Malherbe, N. (2018). Expanding conceptions of liberation: Holding Marxisms with liberation psychology. *Theory & Psychology,* 28(3), 340–357.

Malherbe, N. (2023). Psychology and the question of radical democracy. *Theory & Psychology,* 33(6), 771–791.

Malherbe, N. (2024). A psychoanalytic case for anti-capitalism as an organisational form. *Theory, Culture & Society,* 41(6), 77–94.

Malherbe, N., & Canham, H. (2024). Reading a liberation psychology archive in South Africa. *South African Journal of Psychology,* 54(4), 475–487.

Malherbe, N., Ratele, K., Adams, G., Reddy, G., & Suffla, S. (2021). A decolonial Africa (n)-centered psychology of antiracism. *Review of General Psychology,* 25(4), 437–450.

Mamdani, M. (2012). *Define and rule: Native as political identity.* Harvard University Press.

Manganyi, C. (2018). Making strange: Race science and ethnopsychiatric discourse. *Psychology in Society,* 57, 4–23.

Manganyi, N. C. (2019 [1973]). *Being-black-in-the-world.* Wits University Press.

Martín-Baró, I. (1994). *Writings for a liberation psychology:*Harvard University Press.

Marx, K. (1973). *Grundrisse: Foundations of the critique of political economy.* Penguin.

Marx, K. & Engels, F. (1978). The German ideology: Part I. In R. C. Tucker (ed.), *The Marx–Engels reader* (pp. 146–200). Norton.

Memmi, A. (2013). *The colonizer and the colonized.* Routledge.

Merhej, R., & Makarem, R. (2025). The impact of neoliberalism on psychological research and practice. *Theory & Psychology*, 35(1), 78–97.

Mitchell, J. (1971). *Women's estate.* Penguin.

Mitchell, J. (1973). *Psychoanalysis and feminism.* Vintage Books.

Moane, G. (2003). Bridging the personal and the political: Practices for a liberation psychology. *American Journal of Community Psychology*, 31, 91–101.

Moghaddam, F. M. (2010). Commentary: Intersubjectivity, interobjectivity, and the embryonic fallacy in developmental science. *Culture & Psychology*, 16(4), 465–475.

Montero, M. (1998). Psychosocial community work as an alternative mode of political action (The construction and critical transformation of society). *Community, Work & Family*, 1(1), 65–78.

Montero, M., Sonn, C. C., & Burton, M. (2017). Community psychology and liberation psychology: A creative synergy for an ethical and transformative praxis. In M. A. Bond, I. Serrano-García, C. B. Keys, & M. Shinn (eds), *APA handbook of community psychology* (vol. 1, pp. 149–167). American Psychological Association.

More, M. P. (2021). Chabani Manganyi: Existential phenomenological psychology of difference. *Alternation*, 38, 95–121.

Morris, B. (2022). Strange bedfellows: Psychoanalytic theory's place in critical psychology. *Awry: Journal of Critical Psychology*, 3(1), 1–5.

Nunes, R. (2021). *Neither vertical nor horizontal: A theory of political organization.* Verso.

Oladejo, A. O., Malherbe, N., & van Niekerk, A. (2024). Climate justice, capitalism, and the political role of the psychological professions. *Review of General Psychology*, 28(1), 3–16.

Parker, I. (2007). *Revolution in psychology: Alienation to emancipation.* Pluto Press.

Parker, I. (2011). *Lacanian psychoanalysis: Revolutions in subjectivity.* Routledge.

Parker, I. (2014). *Psychology after psychoanalysis: Psychosocial studies and beyond.* Routledge.

Parker, I. (2018). Psychoanalytic clinical case presentations, the case against. *Lacunae: APPI International Journal for Lacanian Psychoanalysis*, 17, 6–36.

Parker, I. (2022). For a people's history of psychoanalysis. Retrieved from https://anticapitalistresistance.org/for-a-peoples-history-of-psychoanalysis.

Parker, I., & Pavón-Cuéllar, D. (2021). *Psychoanalysis and revolution: Critical psychology for liberation movements.* 1968 Press.

Pavón-Cuéllar, D. (2017). *Marxism and psychoanalysis: In or against psychology?* Routledge.

Pavón-Cuéllar, D., & González Equihua, E. E. (2013). Subversive psychoanalysis and its potential orientation toward a liberation psychology: From a Lacanian reading of Martín-Baró to a committed use of Jacques Lacan. *Theory & Psychology*, 23(5), 639–656.

Popa, B. (2018). Shame and cognitive strikes: What would it "really" mean for queer psychoanalysis to enter the perverse?. *Studies in Gender and Sexuality*, 19(2), 145–156.

Prempeh, E. O. K. (2004). Anti-globalization forces, the politics of resistance, and Africa: Promises and perils. *Journal of Black Studies*, 34(4), 580–598.

Rada, M. (2022). Overdetermined: Psychoanalysis and solidarity. *Differences*, 33(2–3), 1–32.

Ratele, K. (2019). *The world looks like this from here: Thoughts on African psychology.* Wits University Press.

Ratele, K., Malherbe, N., Cornell, J., Day, S., Helman, R., Makama, R., Titi, N., Suffla, S., & Dlamini, S. (2020). Elaborations on (a) decolonising Africa(n)-centred feminist psychology. *Psychology in Society*, 59, 1–19.

Rivera, E. T. (2020). Concepts of liberation psychology. In L. Comas-Díaz & E. Torres Rivera (eds), *Liberation psychology: Theory, method, practice & social justice* (pp. 41–52). American Psychological Association.

Roberts, R. (2015). *Psychology and capitalism: The manipulation of mind*. Zero Books.

Robinson, P. A. (1969) *The Freudian left: Wilhelm Reich, Geza Roheim, Herbert Marcuse*. Harper and Row.

Rose, N. (1985). *The psychological complex: Psychology, politics and society in England 1869–1939*. Routledge and Kegan Paul.

Rousselle, D., & Evren, S. (eds). (2011). *Post-anarchism: A reader*. Pluto Press.

Rustin, M. (1982). A socialist consideration of Kleinian psychoanalysis. *New Left Review*, 131(1), 71–96.

Saketopoulou, A., & Pellegrin, A. (2023). *Gender without identity*. Unconscious in Translation.

Schabas, M. (2007). *The natural origins of economics*. University of Chicago Press.

Seedat, M. (1997). The quest for liberatory psychology. *South African Journal of Psychology*, 27 (4), 261–270.

Seedat, M., & Suffla, S. (2017). Community psychology and its (dis)contents, archival legacies and decolonisation. *South Africa Journal of Psychology*, 47(4), 421–443.

Seedat, M., Suffla, S., & Christie, D. J. (eds). (2017). *Emancipatory and participatory methodologies in peace, critical, and community psychology*. Springer.

Shalhoub-Kevorkian, N. (2020). Gun to body: Mental health against unchilding. *International Journal of Applied Psychoanalytic Studies*, 17(2), 126–145.

Sheehi, L. (2024). Intent to harm: Settler colonial outposts in psychoanalysis. *Middle East Critique*, 33(3), 419–434.

Sheehi, L., & Sheehi, S. (2022). *Psychoanalysis under occupation: Practicing resistance in Palestine*. Routledge.

Sheehi, S., & Sheehi, L. (2023). The reverie of resistance. *Psychotherapy & Politics International*, 21(3–4), 1–6.

Sheehi, S., & Sheehi, L. (2024). The colonial republic of psychoanalysis: how psychoanalysis polices the psychic sovereignty of "Others". *Psychoanalysis, Culture & Society*, 1–20.

Simpson, L. B. (2017). *As we have always done: Indigenous freedom through radical resistance*. University of Minnesota Press.

Solnit, R. (2016). *Hope in the dark: Untold histories, wild possibilities*. Haymarket Books.

Sonn, C. C., Fernández, J. S., MouraJr., J. F., Madyaningrum, M. E., & Malherbe, N. (eds). (2024). *Handbook of decolonial community psychology*. Springer.

Stavrakakis, Y. (2007). *The Lacanian left: Psychoanalysis, theory, and politics*. Edinburgh University Press.

Stevens, G. (2020). Racial alienation, the (im)possibilities of resolution, and the absent/present Other: Venxing vantage points from the patient/trainee: A discussion of 'racial difference, rupture, and repair: A view from the couch and back. *Psychoanalytic Dialogues*, 30(6), 716–722.

Tissaw, M. A., & Osbeck, L. M. (2007). On critical engagement with the mainstream: Introduction. *Theory & Psychology*, 17(2), 155–168.

Timpanaro, S. (2011). *The Freudian slip: Psychoanalysis and textual criticism*. Verso.

Tomšič, S. (2015). *Capitalist unconscious: Marx and Lacan*. Verso.

Tupinambá, G. (2021). *The desire of psychoanalysis: Exercises in Lacanian thinking.* Northwestern University Press.

Valdés, A. (2022). *Toward a feminist Lacanian left: Psychoanalytic theory and intersectional politics.* Routledge.

Volpato, C. (2000). Italian race psychology during fascism. *European Bulletin of Social Psychology,* 12(2), 4–13.

Wark, M. (2022). Dear cis analysts: A call for reparations. Retrieved from www.parap raxismagazine.com/articles/dear-cis-analysts.

Watkins, M., & Shulman, H. (2008). *Toward psychologies of liberation.* Palgrave Macmillan.

Weisstein, N. (1993). Psychology constructs the female; or the fantasy life of the male psychologist (with some attention to the fantasies of his friends, the male biologist and the male anthropologist). *Feminism & Psychology,* 3(2), 194–210.

Winston, A. S. (2020). Why mainstream research will not end scientific racism in psychology. *Theory & Psychology,* 30(3), 425–430.

Wright, E. O. (2019). *How to be an anti-capitalist in the 21st century.* Verso.

Chapter 2

Liberating Fantasy

Introduction

In his landmark work on liberation psychology, Martín-Baró (1994) explored how continuous trauma can lead people to retreat into fantasy which may, in turn, culminate in paranoid symptoms. However, when we take a longer view of the liberation psychology tradition, we see that fantasy appears only sporadically within this tradition. As such, psychoanalytic liberation psychology practitioners concerned with fantasy must turn to how fantasy has been engaged within progressive psychoanalytic scholarship. It is then with psychoanalytic insights into fantasy that liberation psychology might become useful to anti-capitalist activists concerned with the political valances of fantasy.

In what follows, I offer a brief overview of the psychoanalytic conceptions of fantasy most pertinent to this chapter's arguments, giving particular focus to the Lacanian theory of fantasy. Following this, I consider how we can understand political fantasy by looking at what constitutes capitalist and anti-capitalist fantasies. I then turn to my own psychoanalytic liberation psychology work with a South African anti-capitalist social movement, whose political activity is undergirded by a bricolage of fantasies, breakdowns in fantasy, and holding reality accountable to liberatory fantasies. I conclude by speculating on what fantasy could mean for future psychoanalytic liberation psychology work.

Psychoanalytic Conceptions of Fantasy

In common parlance, fantasy denotes an imagined or hallucinatory image that stands opposed to reality (Daly, 1999). Fantasy is what the subject wishes from reality. Psychoanalytic theory, however, posits that fantasy forms part of the subject's reality (Freud, 1989 [1911]). The desires that we stage in fantasy determine the symbolic structure (i.e. the systems of signs and symbols that we are born into; Leader, 2008) on which we rely to make sense of reality. More specifically, fantasy offers the subject an imagined origin

DOI: 10.4324/9781003612728-2

point – or a libidinally charged narrative frame (Sánchez, 2024) – which covers over tension, contradiction, and the unrepresentable facets of subjectivity (Daly, 1999). In the contradiction-free scene provided by fantasy, subjects position themselves in relation to desire (Laplanche & Pontalis, 1968). However, as Žižek (1997) insists, we do not desire a particular object. Indeed, desire is structured ambivalently (Sánchez, 2024). Thus, it is fantasy that surrounds the object that we desire. It is not a higher wage that workers desire, but the fantasy of the life that a higher wage will bring them. It is, therefore, in fantasy that we are given readable images that explain to us why things are the way that they are, how we would like things to be, and, indeed, how we would like them not to be (Glynos, 2008). In these ways, we can understand fantasy as operating "in a fictional direction" (Shajirat, 2020, p. 320).

Although Freud (1989 [1911]) believed that fantasy could form part of conscious thought, such as daydreaming, he was more preoccupied with fantasy as an unconscious phenomenon (Sharpe & Turner, 2019), wherein traumatic and repressed points of reference become concealed (Žižek, 1997). However, conscious-unconscious distinctions are not always clear in the fantasy frame. While there are some psychoanalytic thinkers (such as those working in the Kleinian tradition) who differentiate unconscious *phantasy* from conscious *fantasy* (Behagel & Mert, 2021), I tend to agree with Laplanche and Pontalis (1968), who argue against this distinction simply because the fantasy frame is always shifting. The subject may well come to repress conscious fantasy, rendering it unconscious. It is, therefore, more useful to think of fantasy as forged through a continuous conscious-unconscious dialectical psychic process.

Lacan's "return to Freud" via structural linguistics has proven especially influential for understanding the role that fantasy plays in the development of human subjectivity in situ. To understand what Lacan meant by fantasy, we must first understand what he meant by subjectivity. For Lacan (1992), the subject cannot be definitively known because it is continually being thought and elucidated through a continuous configuration of signs, such as language. The signs through which we construct our subjectivity are far from stable. Signs are also external to the subject, meaning that subjects are open to being divided, misinterpreted, and inhabited by the outside world (Parker & Pavón-Cuéllar, 2021). It is because we are reproduced through the contradictions and splits inherent to signs that the subject is never entirely accessed by or integrated into a given symbolic order (Malherbe, 2024). It is here, in this non-deterministic psychic space, that we find fantasy. The sequence of images which make up the fantasy scene conceals from the subject the splits inherent to subjectivity (Laplanche & Pontalis, 1968). The fantasy, in other words, covers over the subject's inability to cohere with a given symbolic order. This protects the subject from feelings of anxiety and uncertainty while, at the same time, stages desire (Sharpe & Turner, 2019).

Subjectivity is, by and large, dispersed around the fantasy scene, with a single subject taking up any number of identities, actions, and subject positions within a fantasy (Butler, 1990).

Lacan (1992, p. 184) posited that a central function of fantasy is to organise our enjoyment. By enjoyment, he meant an excessive sort of "pleasurable suffering" where unconscious pleasure is derived from certain kinds of pain (Stavrakakis, 1999). Thus, we can think of enjoyment as an exhilarating, transgressive pleasure that can only be experienced momentarily (Daly, 1999). We tend to enjoy through excess or loss (Lacan, 1992). Defying authority, transgressing social mores, and giving ourselves over to a cause can all bring about a sense of enjoyment. How convincing or desirable a fantasy is depends on how it stages the subject's capturing or recapturing of enjoyment (Glynos & Stavrakakis, 2008). It is through impossible promises of complete enjoyment that fantasy *grips* the subject at the psychic level (Glynos, 2008).

Lacan (1992, p. 71) insisted that fantasy is at once external and intimate, "something strange to me, although it is at the heart of me". Fantasies are, in this sense, objectively subjective (Žižek, 1997). It is because fantasies speak so directly to our individual and social enmeshments that it is difficult to abandon the fantasy frame altogether. We can, however, loosen fantasy's psychic grip. Lacan (1992) spoke of this loosening as a traversal of the fantasy, whereby the subject encircles a fantasy without repressing or exiting from it entirely, thereby recognising and taking responsibility for the kinds of enjoyment staged in fantasy. To engage critically with how fantasy informs and grips subjectivity is, then, to consider the ethical, and therefore also the political, valances of fantasy.

Political Fantasy

Behagel and Mert (2021) posit that a fantasy is political when it creates a split between a political object and a political subject. It is within this split that the subject invests in fantasies which stage desires for the obstacles that must be overcome or the objects that must be attained to guarantee complete political mastery and enjoyment (Glynos & Stavrakakis, 2008). While political fantasies might look to the future or the past when staging desire (Newman, 2011), like all fantasies, they transgress established social norms, with little space for contradiction and ambiguity.

The clear, non-contradictory narrative that fantasy provides to our symbolic universe means that fantasy allies closely with ideology. Where ideology attempts to explain the subject's loss of enjoyment, fantasy provides solutions (always deferred) for regaining enjoyment and overcoming subjective splitting (Sharpe & Turner, 2019). Fantasy delineates what or who must be eliminated, defeated, or overcome for the subject to reconcile with themselves and the world (Daly, 1999). Right-wing fantasies, for example, render a particular – usually marginalised – othered subject (e.g. foreign nationals, the poor, ethnic minorities) responsible for structural inequities like unemployment and precarity. For the liberal, it is the intolerant subject that prevents us from realising the (structurally impossible) fantasy of a moderate capitalism without mass poverty. And for those of us on the anti-capitalist Left, it is often the fantasy of a defeated Right that promises to solve the problems internal to our movements, such as fracturing or unchecked prejudice. In each of these examples, ideological enemies are made responsible for a non-realised mode of enjoyment staged in fantasy. The continual drive to realise the enjoyment and/or ontological security promised by fantasy is what secures the subject's psychic investment in ideology (Behagel & Mert, 2021; Kabgani & Clarke, 2017).

It is because political fantasies are constituted by ideologies, languages, and myths that they are always, to some degree, shared (see Dolar, 2008). In studying political fantasy, we can begin to understand how the outside gets inside of us, so to speak (Sánchez, 2024). Empirical psychoanalytic research has sought to examine the role of political fantasy in workplace practices (for a useful overview see Glynos, 2008) and social movement settings (e.g. Sánchez, 2024; Williams et al., 2025). There have also been philosophical and literary treatises that draw from psychoanalytic conceptions of fantasy to understand different political phenomena, such as the state, capitalism, racism, patriarchy, and colonialism (e.g. Aretxaga, 2003; Behagel & Mert, 2021; Johanssen, 2021; Kabgani & Clarke, 2017; Rose, 1998; Shajirat, 2020). Moreover, some psychoanalysts have undertaken the reflexive work of engaging with the fantasies that practitioners bring into the clinic, and how these fantasies risk mirroring oppressive socio-political structures (Weisstein, 1993). For instance, in examining psychoanalytic conceptions of trauma, Saketopoulou (2023) has interrogated fantasies of psychological repair that many analysts and analysands invest in psychoanalytic treatment, asking what these fantasies can tell us about the broader political structures in and by which they are constituted. In their work in Palestine, Sheehi and Sheehi (2022) evoke what they refer to as psychoanalytic innocence, which we can understand as the fantasies of political neutrality harnessed by psychoanalytic practitioners to disavow their complicity in settler colonialism.

All political projects rely on the desires and identifications staged in fantasy. The politics of political fantasy are thus determined by the attitude or position that a subject takes up in relation to that fantasy (Newman, 2011). Although there are many kinds of political fantasy, I am primarily concerned in this chapter with what fantasy means for grassroots anti-capitalist movements. However, to develop a suitably dialectical understanding of the anti-capitalist fantasy, we must first outline what it is we mean by capitalist fantasy.

Capitalist Fantasy

Under capitalism, unconscious desire becomes wrapped up with the imperatives of capital. Desire is, in other words, confined to a symbolic order premised on dehumanising and uneven modes of consumption and (re)production (see Saketopoulou, 2023). When we cede our desires to capital in this way, we turn away from them and, consequentially, feel guilty (Lacan, 1992). It follows, then, that capitalism's hold over and distortions of our desire influence the fantasy frame, ensuring that the subject's fantasmatic transgression adheres to the logic of capital. Put differently, under capitalism, setting a fantasy in motion often means committing to the ideological premises of capitalism (e.g. ruthless and individualised competition; fabulous wealth; ownership) by transgressing officially sanctioned norms (e.g. law, basic humanity, respectability). Capitalism thus determines not only how the subject invests in fantasy, but also what is possible and what is mere fantasy (Harney & Moten, 2013).

The desires staged within capitalism's fantasy frames (e.g. upward mobility; more commodities; better commodities; job satisfaction; success over market competitors; protection for the nuclear family) often represent the desire for basic survival and the promise of a better life (Ruti, 2008). Desires like these are desirable because they do not deliver the enjoyment and/or the wholeness that they promise, leaving us to continually grasp at them. Our psychic investment in capital depends on the suspension of enjoyment, that is, on the unrealisable nature of capitalist desires (see McGowan, 2022). In this way, we develop neurotic attachments to, and even psychically invest in, capitalism's symbolic social order (Malherbe, 2024).

To invest psychically in the capitalist fantasy does not necessarily mean that every subject consciously believes that capitalism will deliver harmony, completeness, or permanent enjoyment. The material conditions in which the vast majority of people live refute capital's promises of a better life. Yet, people are by material necessity compelled to act in accordance with the capitalist fantasy; to behave as if they believe in capital's fantasmatic scenes. This is what Marx (1977, p. 899) referred to as the "silent compulsion of economic relations". Curiously, then, it is often when we assume a minimal, critical distance from a fantasy that we invest most strongly in it. For example, the worker might commit to doing the best job possible within capitalist institutions whose exploitative nature they openly acknowledge, thereby living out fantasies of individual mastery or heroism over these flawed institutions (Glynos, 2008). In an anecdotal example provided by Žižek (1997), some of the most ruthlessly committed soldiers are those who subvert the official militaristic order in small ways (e.g. mocking its daily rituals). From these ultimately inconsequential subversions, a soldier's dissident energies are placated through crumbs of enjoyment that leave the broader militaristic system unchallenged. In both of these examples, capitalist fantasy speaks not to the subject's conscious wishes, but to unconscious attachments to and investments in the knowledges and beliefs that define the capitalist symbolic order (Butler, 1990; Žižek, 1997). Even if we consciously denounce capitalism, our fantasies can reveal unconscious attachments to and investments in political, economic, and cultural horizons of possibility that are determined by capital.

Our psychic investment in capitalism is also harnessed through fantasies of liberal agency (Saketopoulou, 2023). Within these fantasies, freedom is confined to a marketised logic (e.g. freedom to consume; freedom to work; freedom to exploit or compete with others), wherein the consistency of the capitalist symbolic order depends on subjects making some of the choices available to them, but not others (Žižek, 1997). The violent manner by which several US university administrations have responded to student-led Palestinian solidarity encampments since 2024 serves as an example of when people act on an implicitly barred choice that cannot be tolerated by those invested in maintaining the seeming coherence of the capitalist order. In 2012, the South African state murdered 34 miners who exercised their legal – and thus officially sanctioned, but unofficially barred – choice to strike. These miners exited, and thus exposed the inadequacies of, fantasies of liberal agency, and they were punished by state capitalist powers for doing so.

The scapegoating fantasy represents another way by which subjects psychically invest in the capitalist social order. The racist subject tolerates violent exploitation and expropriation by locating the source of this violence not in the structures and institutions of capital accumulation, but in a racialised Other. Put differently, the racist fantasy creates an imagined racialised threat to social and subjective harmony (a threat that is always tied in with racist desire; see Fanon, 1986 [1967]; Saketopoulou, 2023), with both quotidian and spectacular racism responding to this threat (Rodríguez, 2015). McGowan (2022) insists that subjects invested in the racist fantasy consciously believe that the racialised Other represents an obstacle to enjoyment. However, at the unconscious level, the racialised Other serves as a vehicle for racist enjoyment. The symbolic consistency of racist subjectivity is thus affirmed by fantasies of a threat, embodied in an imagined racialised Other, to this consistency (Daly, 1999). We can, in this respect, observe how fantasies of purity, wholeness, and mastery that are attached to whiteness (and that, in a racial capitalist order, are affirmed through the material privileges attached to whiteness) can result in whiteness being essentialised, violently defended, and closed off from contradiction or change (Saketopoulou, 2023; Sheehi & Sheehi, 2020). We should not, then, understand racist fantasy as an aberration from capitalist ideology, but as constitutive of the psychic apparatuses of coloniality upon which capital accumulation has always relied (Shajirat, 2020).

The scapegoating fantasy also operates on the national level (Verma, 2004). The capitalist state relies on a set of fantasmatic investments that ignore or perpetuate imagined threats to state cohesion (Aretxaga, 2003). It is because these threats are imaginary that they retain an anxiety-producing paranoic psychic grip – the feeling that although they are not realised in any observable way, they could come to fruition at any moment (Žižek, 1997). The state provides "unspoken components of social belonging" (Rose, 1998,

p. 6) by locating the solutions to shared social problems in fantasies of mass incarceration, liberal democracy, war, imperial extraction, violent policing, and austerity (see Verma, 2004). Moreover, politicians in the United States, the United Kingdom, South Africa, Brazil, India, and many other places routinely identify foreign nationals, rather than a rapacious commitment to finance capital, as impeding national development. We also see fantasies, circulated by states, of a recuperated wholeness that is to be found in traditional morality (Butler, 1990). Exemplary of this are the queerphobic, transphobic, and anti-abortion legislations being passed all over the world. The scapegoating fantasies on which the capitalist state depends are, in short, harnessed to consolidate various statist fantasies, including "the fantasy of statehood, the fantasy of total control, the fantasy of appropriation of the other, the fantasy of heterosexual domesticity" (Aretxaga, 2003, p. 402).

On the global scale, imperialist intervention relies on a particular fantasy that, in repressing histories of colonial plunder, stages the desire to save the Global South from perpetual civil war, social backwardness, and/or a premodern past into which it is apparently frozen (Shajirat, 2020). Yeğenoğlu (1998) demonstrates how, for instance, the hijab has served as a singular image onto which imperial fantasies of nationalism, saviourism, and control are projected (see also Ghannam, 2005). Such fantasies have clear material consequences, but they also have epistemological consequences, as noted in colonial museums, Eurocentric teaching curricula, official (fundamentally colonial) archives, and media depictions that fetishise poverty and resilience in the Global South (see Singh, 2009).

From what has been discussed so far, we can observe how the capitalist fantasy conceals, represses, or denies humanity. This is especially clear in colonial fantasies that justify imperial and racist violence by negating the consciousness and desires of colonised subjects and relegating colonised subjectivity to what Fanon (1986 [1967]) called the zone of nonbeing. We also see a denial of the human within capitalist economic relations. In his mature writings, Marx (1977, p. 165) demonstrates how fantasies tied in with the commodity – the commodity being "the fantastic form of a relation between things" – conceal the violent processes of exploitation and expropriation which bring commodities into existence under capitalism. More recently, Harney and Moten (2013) have argued that fantasies of self-enhancement and mobility reduce the human subject to investment-prone, non-relational pieces of finance capital that are to be managed in accordance with imperial market norms (see also Malherbe, 2024). When cast in this fantasy frame, the human subject is "to feel without emotion, to move without friction, to adapt without question, to translate without pause, to desire without purpose, to connect without interruption" (Harney & Moten, 2013, p. 87). This is, par excellence, the capitalist fantasy of the perfectly known, managed, and surveilled subject. It is a fantasy that serves to conceal the antagonisms and contradictions that mark (inter)subjectivity under capitalism, such as class struggle (Žižek, 1997), the interdependence of productive and reproductive labour (Harney & Moten, 2013), the entwinement of nature and society (Behagel & Mert, 2021), and how exploitation in the capitalist core depends on expropriation and hyper-exploitation in the colonial periphery (Shajirat, 2020). However, because human subjectivity is marked by contradiction, it cannot be wholly symbolised or hailed by capital. As such, human subjects are never entirely determined by capitalism's symbolic order. There are always possibilities for resistance within this order.

Psychoanalytic Liberation Psychology, Anti-Capitalism, and Fantasy

Sánchez (2024, p. 425) writes that "we should pay due attention to the fantasmatic organisation of all kinds of identifications, including the ones with emancipatory events or ideals". Indeed, if fantasy is central to capitalism, it is also fundamental to anti-capitalist emancipation. Different anti-capitalist movements have always attached conceptions of and desires for liberation to different modes of fantasy (see Williams et al., 2025). Socialism might even be thought of as an attempt to act upon the fantasies of freedom structurally disallowed by capitalism's symbolic order. As Marx wrote in an 1844 letter: "the world has long since dreamed of something of which it needs only to become conscious for it to possess it in reality" (Marx & Engels, 1975, p. 144). Feminist consciousness-raising groups are similarly attuned to questions of fantasy and what it means to think outside of a patriarchal capitalist order (Mitchell, 1971). Fantasies of the not-yet-real are, certainly, central to feminist movements (see Butler, 1990), for whom fantasy has represented a right, a freedom, a means to radicalise the political imagination, and a shared performance (Nash, 2014). Fantasy is also fundamental to anti-colonial resistance (see e.g. Kelley, 2002), including decolonising aesthetic traditions that seek to expand the decolonial imaginary while, at the same time, unsettling the violent boundaries imposed and policed by colonising powers (Safaeyan, 2022).

It would seem, then, that anti-capitalists do not need psychoanalytic liberation psychology to engage critically with fantasy. On the contrary, as discussed in Chapter 1, political radicals often regard psychology and psychoanalysis with a justifiable degree of hostility on account of both disciplines aligning, in many respects, with the dictates of capital (see also Christinaki & Sheehi, 2023). Nonetheless, as noted earlier, psychoanalytic liberation psychology can be of use to anti-capitalists when it is evoked and adapted within and for social movements, rather than imposed onto them. Psychoanalytic liberation psychology can, for instance, be drawn upon to facilitate spaces wherein activists engage freely and openly with the psycho-political valances of fantasy.

For those working within the psychoanalytic liberation psychology tradition, attempting to evaluate the politics of a particular fantasy produces little political value. This is because the fantasy scene shifts between conscious and unconscious plains of thought – between known political commitments and unknown desires (see Laplanche & Pontalis, 1968). It is thus more fruitful to consider what the desires staged in fantasy mean for advancing anti-capitalist struggle, and how fantasy can push activists beyond the symbolic limits of the capitalist order, revealing alternative political imaginaries and arrangements of meaning which have been deemed *mere fantasy* by capitalism's ideological forces (Behagel & Mert, 2021).

In her engagement with the regressive and emancipatory possibilities of fantasy, Ruti (2008) outlines two useful categories of fantasy: imaginative and unconscious. Unconscious fantasy, she argues, covers over our subjective lack with ego-affirming visions of the self that take their coordinates from the prevailing capitalist symbolic order. The unconscious fantasy supports capitalism by foreclosing enjoyment and desire within the limits of this order. By contrast, imaginative fantasy pushes the subject to see the world in different ways, loosening the grip that capitalism holds over our political imaginations. It is in imaginative fantasy that the subject can distinguish desire from what is demanded by capitalism (Malherbe, 2024). Imaginative fantasy can call into question capitalism's orthodox unconscious fantasies, and in this, evoke a kind of reflexivity that invigorates the subject (see Sánchez, 2024). To be clear, Ruti's (2008) fantasy categories do not ask us to reify our conception of fantasy as either imaginative or unconscious. Instead, we are compelled to understand fantasy as moving between and through both categories. To borrow from the formulation of Glynos (2008): where unconscious fantasy offers enjoyment located in ideological closure and the guilt associated with transgression, imaginative fantasy inheres a mode of enjoyment associated with an ethical openness linked to exploring the possibilities and desires that exist in contingent encounters.

Imaginative fantasy offers a useful place to begin the work of psychoanalytic liberation psychology. Practitioners can work with activists to facilitate spaces wherein different imaginative fantasies are discussed in relation to the broader political goals of the collective. Within these spaces, not every professed fantasy will align with an emancipatory political program. There is likely to be antagonism between comrades, especially when particular fantasies are understood as regressive, competing with one another, or incompatible (see Williams et al., 2025). Nonetheless, spaces of this kind also hold the potential to transform the symbolic coordinates of different fantasies through the ethos and goals of the anti-capitalist collective while, at the same time, transforming the collective through a bricolage of emancipatory fantasies. The anti-capitalist form is, after all, defined by its ability to institutionalise the unrelenting desires of the subjects that comprise this form (see Stavrakakis, 1999). To openly discuss imaginative fantasies in the context of the anti-capitalist collective is, therefore, not to seek out the fantasy scene that will secure an imagined state of enjoyment, nor is it to determine the collective's agreed-upon fantasmatic limit (see Saketopoulou, 2023). It is, instead, to provoke the kinds of emancipatory desires that encircle different fantasy frames, and to forge commitments to pushing reality to reflect as many of these fantasies as possible (Parker & Pavón-Cuéllar, 2021).

To stretch and hold accountable individual fantasies within and through the anti-capitalist collective represents an attempt to strengthen the solidarity bond through the therapeutic encounter; to consolidate the anti-capitalist form by attending to comrades' differential wounding. Here, psychoanalytic liberation psychology does not seek to eliminate trauma by privileging fantasies of liberation, but is instead drawn upon as a resource for engaging with trauma and fantasy (see Parker & Pavón-Cuéllar, 2021; Saketopoulou, 2023). For instance, by taking seriously how Black and Indigenous subjectivities are degraded and obliterated by colonial capitalism, the anti-capitalist collective is able to surface and institutionalise into its formations different decolonising fantasies (see Sheehi & Sheehi, 2020). To share in the vulnerabilities and emancipatory fantasies of differently wounded subjects can, in turn, enable solidaristic forms of connection that are not burdened by imperatives to fully understand or comprehensively know one's comrades (Saketopoulou, 2023).

Newman's (2004, 2011) critiques of revolutionary fantasy are useful for psychoanalytic liberation psychology work with anti-capitalist movements. Revolutionary fantasies of complete or total liberation, he argues, promise to deliver us from any and all antagonism, thereby releasing subjects from the responsibility to reflect on their political commitments. Saketopoulou (2023, p. 123) similarly warns that political projects driven by "restored freedom and … complete psychic emancipation are fantastical constructions existing only in the minds of those who are unwilling to concede that trauma has irremediable scarring effects". Although anti-capitalist fantasy can offer a degree of hope or respite, it is important not to look away from how such fantasy can foreclose real-world political action by repeatedly deferring to an all-encompassing imaginative event that never arrives. To move away from fantasies of this sort, Newman (2004) insists on bringing fantasies of anti-capitalist revolution to bear on the materiality of our quotidian lives, thereby reconstituting revolution through multiple, insurrectionary, and autonomous ways of life that build anti-capitalist power at a remove from the capitalist state (e.g. worker cooperatives; socialised reproductive labour; community gardens; the ecological commons). Revolutionary fantasies can also be distributed throughout social movement organising (e.g. via non-hierarchical communication structures, equally dividing reproductive labour within movement spaces, and radically democratising decision-making processes). Psychoanalytic liberation psychology practitioners are urged to engage with how revolutionary fantasy grounded in the everyday makes available new ways of life, modalities of relating, intersubjective intensities, and orders of signification, all of which allow us to figure our desires and fantasies in opposition to symbolic orders of capitalist respectability (see Harney &

Moten, 2013). To disperse fantasy through everyday life and political organisation quells the pressure to enjoy in the name of capital accumulation,
and thus returns us to ourselves and our desires through a sense of what
Saketopoulou (2023) calls self-sovereignty.

As important as imaginative fantasies are to anti-capitalist movement-
building, unconscious fantasies should not go unattended. To neglect those
aspects of the anti-capitalist subject that unconsciously identify with capitalism is to miss an opportunity to confront capital's psychic grip, and the
strength that this grip attains when it goes unspoken (Glynos, 2008). In their
research on worker cooperatives, Byrne and Healy (2006) found that open
communication prevents antagonism from being repressed into fantasies of
exclusion and entitlement. Accordingly, psychoanalytic liberation psychology
can be harnessed to establish reflective, agonistic spaces wherein activists
engage with and begin the impossible work of symbolising unconscious
fantasy. It is in attempting to encircle the unknowability of unconscious fantasy
that subjects can move towards formulating a logic of relations and
connections around this fantasy, suspending its efficacy and opening up
possibilities to take responsibility for their unconscious enjoyment (see
McGowan, 2022; Stavrakakis, 1999). Fantasy is, in this way, opened up to
contingency and political resignification, with struggles between fantasies
abandoned for a struggle to relate differently to fantasy (Glynos, 2008).

Commenting on the German Peasants' War, Engels (1965, p. 46) wrote
that "the anticipation of communism nurtured by fantasy became in reality
an anticipation of modern bourgeois conditions". When we ignore the effects
that material reality has on fantasy, he seems to say, we risk unconsciously
ceding the symbolic coordinates of fantasy to the hegemonic capitalist order.
As such, Harney and Moten (2013) insist on advancing emancipatory fantasy from within the hold that colonial capitalism has on both reality and
fantasy. Those working in the psychoanalytic liberation psychology paradigm
are challenged to engage with the material conditions within which fantasies
are formed, while at the same time seeking to understand how the imaginative fantasy frame can be used to destabilise the symbolic constraints of these
conditions. It is thus "in the interstitial spaces between reach and grasp"
(Saketopoulou, 2023, p. 23) that psychoanalytic liberation psychology can be
of use to anti-capitalist movements seeking to engage with fantasy to
consolidate their politics in the face of failure, conflict, disappointment, or
political setback.

Case Reflection

When working with anti-capitalist movements to engage with fantasy, the
psychoanalytic liberation psychology paradigm need not rely on specific
therapeutic interventions or a particular set of psychoanalytic techniques.
Rather, attempts should be made to open up therapeutic spaces in which

fantasy can be explored in a critical but comradely manner (see Sheehi & Sheehi, 2022). Thus, anti-capitalist politics are not vanquished via a retreat into therapy. Therapeutic encounters are, instead, evoked to strengthen the anti-capitalist commitments of the collective, instituting modes of solidarity-building and organisation through reflection and analysis (see Mitchell, 1971).

In what follows, I flesh out some of what has been discussed so far by reflecting on my work with an anti-capitalist movement based in South Africa. The movement is community-led and has, over the last few years, been engaged in street protests as well as formal negotiations with the South African state over sanitation, educational facilities, clean energy, water, housing, municipal services, and dignity. My colleagues and I have collaborated with activists from the movement to produce media products that seek to communicate their struggles to a wider audience and hold space for reflecting on how the movement wages its struggles. In reflecting on this work, I am not concerned with the political content of fantasy, but rather how activists have used fantasy in political ways. As such, and in the interests of preserving anonymity, I do not quote from the activists. Rather, I consider how the collective took up the fantasy frame to assemble a bricolage of fantasies, reconcile with the breakdown of fantasy, and bring fantasy to bear on reality.

Fantasy Bricolage

The South African movement with which my colleagues and I work hosts regular community assemblies. These assemblies have a standing agenda, wherein persistent issues facing the community are discussed, such as housing and sanitation. After every item on the standing agenda has been addressed, community members are invited to discuss struggles that have not yet been articulated.

On the ideological level, these assemblies endeavour to shape the anti-capitalist collective's pragmatic actions (e.g. protests, legislative contestation, state dialogue, militant defence) through the desires that community members stage in different fantasies, such as socialist and feminist revolution, state reform, non-hierarchical governance, religious redemption, Black Consciousness solidarity, and the victory of different – sometimes competing – political parties. In a single community meeting, the anti-capitalist collective moves through these different fantasies, often concluding with prayer and a socialist struggle song from the anti-apartheid era. Here, we observe what I am calling a bricolage of fantasies. Placed within anti-capitalist political formations, the psychic grip of a single fantasy is loosened precisely because it sits alongside several other fantasies, not all of which are compatible with one another. This bricolage of fantasies pushes the anti-capitalist collective to define itself through a range of struggles that are open to contingency (see

Byrne & Healy, 2006). Notably, the different fantasies that constitute the bricolage do not compete for precedence within the movement.

The bricolage of fantasy certainly renders the movement's internal structures vulnerable to divisive ideological currents. The South African state has, at times, seized on some of these internal tensions to sow divisions in the movement (e.g. making promises that it does not intend to fulfil to different fractions in the movement). Moreover, within the movement, tensions that exist between different emancipatory fantasies can and often do make for a highly charged affective atmosphere. However, these tensions rarely collapse into debilitating sorts of political inertia. By repeatedly making space for different anti-capitalist fantasies, community members and movement activists forge movement actions and commitments in relation to the different desires staged in these fantasies. Not every movement activist will identify with or invest in everyone's fantasy of liberation, however, honouring these different fantasies in some way is fundamental to ensuring the movement's legitimacy within the broader community.

My colleagues and I have worked with different movement activists to establish reflective spaces wherein activists and non-activists in the community discuss the perceived limits of fantasy (their own and others) while, at the same time, testing and stretching the possibilities of fantasy. For example, some activists' fantasies of the safety that an increased police presence would bring to their community were tempered by those in the community who argued that security forces in South Africa have, historically, acted to defend property and/or white supremacy. Therefore, the fantasies of safety were not dispelled. Instead, material reality altered these fantasies, which came to stage desires of safety within community-led safety initiatives that operated in the community and autonomously from the state. As such, the bricolage of fantasy became sustained not through the co-existence of static fantasy frames, but through continual engagements guided by the political commitments and analyses of the anti-capitalist collective.

It is also within these reflective spaces that activists work with one another to attend to differential wounding within their movement. The point here is not to resolve tensions that exist between different fantasies of freedom, dignity, and liberation, but to draw out these tensions in order to push the broader movement towards embracing a range of anti-capitalist struggles. For instance, women activists took issue with some of the male leadership for side-lining their struggles around equal education, care work, and safety. In this moment, patriarchal unconscious fantasy was challenged and held accountable to imaginative feminist fantasy. These feminist fantasies were then incorporated into the bricolage of fantasies that defined the anti-capitalist movement (Chapter 4 deals more deeply with some of the complexities of this work). At another meeting, several community members insisted that the movement accounts for the struggles faced by residents in the community with disabilities, including the struggle for safe and reliable transportation routes. Again, the movement's political formation and actions were transformed by accommodating different imaginative fantasies.

Solidarity-building depended in large part on communicating how the movement sought to incorporate different struggles into its various formations, which is to say, how it staged enjoyment through a bricolage of fantasies. Colleagues and I worked with movement activists to produce a short documentary film on the community. The film, which has been screened to other anti-capitalist movements from surrounding communities, repeatedly stresses the importance that different fantasies of anti-capitalist liberation play in guiding the commitments, strategies, tactics, and actions taken by comrades in the movement. As such, the film invites solidarity by showcasing the movement's openness to expanding upon the bricolage of fantasies to which movement activists are committed.

The bricolage of fantasies ensured that movement activists were not animated by or held accountable to a singular fantasy frame. Their waging of anti-capitalist struggle depended on working through avowed differences between comrades, reconciling with contingency, and continually attempting to re-signify movement politics in relation to the ever-evolving bricolage of fantasies. Situated in the gap between the bricolage of fantasies and material reality, my colleagues and I sought to draw upon psychoanalytic liberation psychology to assist activists in communicating the enjoyment of ethical and open-ended anti-capitalist struggle, while also creating spaces for holding and working through movement tensions.

Fantasy Breakdown

While feelings of joy and connection between comrades should not be underplayed within psychoanalytic liberation psychology work, neither should the psychic and material damages incurred in the fight against capitalism (see Proctor, 2024). We can think of the moments of despair and hopelessness within anti-capitalist struggle as resulting in part from a breakdown in fantasy, wherein desires for social transformation seem to dissipate against a backdrop of setbacks, burnouts, and failures. In facing fantasy breakdown, political subjects do not exit one fantasy frame only to enter another. Instead, they enter into a state of mourning. Although mourning is perhaps not immediately generative in any political sense, it is a mainstay within anti-capitalist struggles, serving as affective basis for forging bonds between comrades (see Butler, 2004). It is thus a consequence of colonial capitalist modernity that mourning has been largely exiled from how we understand anti-capitalist struggle (see Gana, 2023).

The anti-capitalist movement with which I have worked in South Africa has experienced several moments of fantasy breakdown. These moments have, for example, occurred in the wake of the state's security forces invading and, in some cases, illegally demolishing shack settlements in the activists' community; the state's continued neglect of the community's basic survival needs like water and electricity; continued antagonism from surrounding communities; internal movement fracturing; and the exhaustion that accompanies waging protracted struggle. Health issues among comrades have also instituted a breakdown in fantasy within the movement. Although experienced in different ways, in general, these moments of fantasy breakdown tend to foreclose desire and the futurity of struggle among movement activists, thereby inhibiting, to varying degrees, their ability to act together.

In our engagements, there have been moments when activists experiencing fantasy breakdown appear unable to emerge from their grief. For many of these activists, the disappointments that accompany the struggles on which their survival depends can feel unbearable. Throughout our discussions, individual activists openly declared their feelings of political hopelessness. These declarations were intensely affective. They were not subject to contestation or debate. Rather, they served as emotional points of connection and mutual holding between comrades. Connecting in this way proved crucial for slowly rebuilding fortitude in the face of fantasy breakdown, which is to say, for instituting a sense of what Proctor (2024) calls patient urgency: a politicised insistence on social transformation which can withstand difficulties, differences, failure, delays, gaps, and interpersonal strains.

For those of us working in the psychoanalytic liberation psychology tradition, a breakdown in fantasy need not compel an urgent return to fantasy, or a rapid working through of despair in the name of continued struggle. There is psychological value in holding and facilitating space for mourning and despair; for an open acknowledgment of shared hardship, traumas, and the personal strains endured in contexts of collective struggle (Saketopoulou, 2023). These spaces are not willed towards repair or adaptation. They are characterised by modes of witnessing and connection facilitated by shared pain.

Following fantasy breakdown, some activists with whom I have worked continue to struggle in a pessimistic mode without the promise of emancipatory fantasy, while others have worked to reconstitute previously held fantasies of liberation. They have continued to wage the struggle against racial capitalism precisely because the survival of their community is dependent on their doing so. This struggle is as relentless as the onslaughts of capital. There is, therefore, a sense of relief – perhaps fleeting, but nonetheless real – to be sought in abandoning resolution and repair for an acknowledgment of the psychic tolls of struggle. For resource-strapped movements, psychoanalytic liberation psychology can be useful for creating spaces like these wherein activists are able to hold and witness the psychic consequences of anti-capitalist struggle.

The breakdown of fantasy indicates to those of us working in the psychoanalytic liberation psychology tradition that we should not fetishise traversing the fantasy. Indeed, there are points at which the fantasy frame cannot hold; when there is no fantasy to traverse. Establishing spaces to mourn the loss of fantasy – spaces that have little or no use for fantasy – can serve as a respite, and an opportunity to connect on an intense, reflective, and affective level with one's comrades through a shared sense of loss and/or mourning. These spaces are not reparative, but they can play a part in building patient urgency among comrades. Mourning is not, as Freud believed, the task of an individual. It is inscribed in communities and can become part of one's duty to their community (Leader, 2008).

Asserting Fantasy onto Reality

Part of the work of anti-capitalist movements is to push material existence to reflect the movement's fantasmatic investments in liberation. Anti-capitalist fantasy can, in other words, be brought to bear on reality in different ways. Asserting the fantasy frame onto reality is not to invest in a complete utopian rupture (see Newman, 2004). It is to realise fragments of a fantasy. Our desires, in turn, encircle these fragments, driving movement activists to realise larger and more fragments.

The anti-capitalist collective with which I work asserts fragments of fantasy onto reality through protests, road blockades, community strikes, lockouts, and other modes of militant action. Other than availing the resources required for organising such action (e.g. venues, communications, transportation), there is little need for psychoanalytic liberation psychology here. Indeed, when it comes to advancing such anti-capitalist action, psychological practitioners are more useful as activist-citizens than they are as practitioners. Nonetheless, there are some anti-capitalist actions to which psychoanalytic liberation psychology can be of use.

Drawing from institutional resources, colleagues and I worked with comrades from this anti-capitalist movement to facilitate a dialogue with the South African state. The dialogue was held at a venue near to the activists' community. After several activists presented their community's grievances to a state representative (with many of these grievances centring on state abandonment and state violence), the discussion quickly became heated. The solutions offered by the state representative were by and large grounded in the immovable symbolic logic of capital. He encouraged activists to lodge their complaints formally through official state communication channels and to follow the protocols that would allow for the kind of state recognition required for effective service delivery in the community. The activists, in response, refused these limited choices grounded in liberal agency. They insisted that if the state did not meet their demands, they would continue asserting fantasies of liberation onto reality via socially disruptive protest action.

The dialogue concluded with activists and the state actor agreeing to establish a communicative forum between the state and community representatives. Although the forum was set up, it was quickly captured by bureaucratic procedural mechanisms that disallowed activists' articulation of liberatory fantasies. As such, activists continue to fight to realise fragments of these fantasies through collective political action, such as protests and blockades, as well as in prefigurative community practices like sustainable subsistence farming, equal education initiatives, and clean energy projects.

There are political limits to the psychoanalytic liberation psychology paradigm, and there are moments when psychological practitioners will need to step outside of this paradigm if they are to be of use to anti-capitalist struggle. Nonetheless, there are certain anti-capitalist engagements for which psychoanalytic liberation psychology can be of use. In the case reflection recounted here, any success resulting from the activists' facilitated dialogue with the state is not immediately clear. However, it is perhaps unhelpful to subject these engagements to such outcome-oriented assessments. The dialogue forms just one element of a protracted anti-capitalist struggle. Indeed, the content and outcome of the dialogue have been used by activists to build solidarity with surrounding communities facing similar struggles against the South African state. The failure of fantasy in one area of anti-capitalist struggle does not mean the failure of struggle as such.

Conclusion

In this chapter, I have attempted to demonstrate that fantasy is a central component of both capitalism and anti-capitalist resistance. In reflecting on my own work, I sought to have made clear some of the ways by which psychoanalytic liberation psychology can serve as a resource for assisting social movement actors in efforts to consolidate their struggles through critical engagements with fantasy.

It is my hope that the shortcomings, oversights, and weak spots of the provocations offered in this chapter are used to bolster and inform future psychoanalytic liberation psychology work. It would perhaps be useful to consider how fantasy intersects with other psychoanalytic concepts (e.g. anxiety; defence mechanisms; symbolic castration; transference), as well as what these intersections mean for acting on the values of liberation psychology (e.g. de-alienation; de-naturalisation; de-ideologisation; problematisation). It is in this way that psychoanalytic liberation psychology can serve as a tool for ensuring that the psychological and the political do not compete within movement spaces, but are instead held together, with each informing our understandings of and engagements with the other.

References

Aretxaga, B. (2003). Maddening states. *Annual Review of Anthropology*, 32(1), 393–410.
Behagel, J. H., & Mert, A. (2021). The political nature of fantasy and political fantasies of nature. *Journal of Language and Politics*, 20(1), 79–94.

Butler, J. (1990). The force of fantasy: Feminism, Mapplethorpe, and discursive excess. *Differences*, 2(2), 105–125.

Butler, J. (2004). *Precarious life: The powers of mourning and violence.* Verso.

Byrne, K. & Healy, S. (2006). Cooperative subjects: Toward a post-fantasmatic enjoyment of the economy. *Rethinking Marxism*, 18(2), 241–258.

Christinaki, A., & Sheehi, L. (2023). The unconscious matters: Sexuality, violence, regimes: A short conversation with Lara Sheehi. *Studies in Gender and Sexuality*, 24(4), 219–225.

Daly, G. (1999). Ideology and its paradoxes: Dimensions of fantasy and enjoyment. *Journal of Political Ideologies*, 4(2), 219–238.

Dolar, M. (2008). Freud and the political. *Unbound*, 4(15), 15–29.

Engels, F. (1965). *The peasant war in Germany.* Progress.

Fanon, F. (1986 [1967]). *Black skin, white masks.* Pluto.

Freud, S. (1989 [1911]). Formulations on the two principles of mental functioning. In P. Gay (ed.), *The Freud reader* (pp. 301–306). Norton.

Gana, N. (2023). *Melancholy acts: Defeat and cultural critique in the Arab world.* Fordham University Press.

Ghannam, J. (2005). The use of psychoanalytic constructs in the service of empire: Comment on Baruch (2003). *Psychoanalytic Psychology*, 22(1), 135–139.

Glynos, J. (2008). Ideological fantasy at work. *Journal of political Ideologies*, 13(3), 275–296.

Glynos, J., & Stavrakakis, Y. (2008). Lacan and political subjectivity: Fantasy and enjoyment in psychoanalysis and political theory. *Subjectivity*, 24, 256–274.

Harney, S., & Moten, F. (2013). *The undercommons: Fugitive planning and Black study.* Minor Compositions.

Johanssen, J. (2021). *Fantasy, online misogyny and the manosphere: Male bodies of dis/inhibition.* Routledge.

Kabgani, S., & Clarke, M. (2017). Fantasy, nostalgia and ideology: A Lacanian reading of post-revolutionary Iran. *Psychoanalysis, Culture & Society*, 22, 154–172.

Kelley, R. D. G. (2002). *Freedom dreams: The Black radical imagination.* Beacon Press.

Lacan, J. (1992). *The ethics of psychoanalysis.* Routledge.

Laplanche, J. & Pontalis, J.-B. (1968). Fantasy and the origins of sexuality. *The International Journal of Psycho-Analysis*, 9, 1–18.

Leader, D. (2008). *The new black: Mourning, melancholia and depression.* Penguin.

Malherbe, N. (2024). Anti-capitalist subjectivity: Considerations of fantasy, (in)action, and solidarity-building. *Subjectivity*, 31(1), 59–78.

Martín-Baró, I. (1994). *Writings for a liberation psychology.* Harvard University Press.

Marx, K. (1977). *Capital: A critique of political economy, vol. 1.* Vintage.

Marx, K., & Engels, F. (1975). *Collected works, vol. 3.* International Publishers.

McGowan, T. (2022). *The racist fantasy: Unconscious roots of hatred.* Bloomsbury.

Mitchell, J. (1971). *Women's estate.* Penguin.

Nash, J. C. (2014). *The black body in ecstasy: Reading race, reading pornography.* Duke University Press.

Newman, S. (2004). Interrogating the master: Lacan and radical politics. *Psychoanalysis, Culture & Society*, 9, 298–314.

Newman, S. (2011). Postanarchism and space: Revolutionary fantasies and autonomous zones. *Planning Theory*, 10(4), 344–365.

Parker, I., & Pavón-Cuéllar, D. (2021). *Psychoanalysis and revolution: Critical psychology for liberation movements.* 1968 Press.

Proctor, H. (2024). *Burnout: The emotional experience of political defeat.* Verso.

Rodríguez, R. T. (2015). Fantasy. *Critical Ethnic Studies,* 1(1), 95–100.

Rose, J. (1998). *States of fantasy.* Oxford University Press.

Ruti, M. (2008). The fall of fantasies: A Lacanian reading of lack. *Journal of the American Psychoanalytic Association,* 56 (2), 483–508.

Safaeyan, S. (2022). Global, decolonial, antiracist, polychromatic: Literary Afrofuturism in the Twenty-First Century. *Science Fiction Film & Television,* 15(1), 93–100.

Saketopoulou, A. (2023). *Sexuality beyond consent: Risk, race, traumatophilia.* New York University Press.

Sánchez, G. (2024). 'Chile woke up' (and I can fall asleep no more): The fantasmatic organisation of the desire for change. *Psychoanalysis, Culture & Society,* 29(3), 412–428.

Shajirat, A. (2020). The colonial mirror of fantasy: Race, gender, and history in Charlotte Smith's The Story of Henrietta (1800) and Sophia Lee's The Recess (1783–85). *The Eighteenth Century,* 61(3), 313–334.

Sharpe, M., & Turner, K. (2019). Fantasy. In Y. Stavrakakis (ed.), *Routledge handbook of psychoanalytic political theory* (pp. 187–271). Routledge.

Sheehi, S., & Sheehi, L. (2020). The settlers' town is a strongly built town: Fanon in Palestine. *International Journal of Applied Psychoanalytic Studies,* 17(2), 183–192.

Sheehi, L., & Sheehi, S. (2022). *Psychoanalysis under occupation: Practicing resistance in Palestine.* Routledge.

Singh, K. (2009). Material fantasy. The museum in colonial India. In G. Sinha (ed.), *Art and visual culture in India 1857–2007* (pp. 40–51). Marg Publications.

Stavrakakis, Y. (1999). *Lacan and the political.* Routledge.

Verma, K. D. (2004). The structure of colonial fantasy. *South Asian Review,* 25(1), 3–15.

Yeğenoğlu, M. (1998). *Colonial fantasies: Towards a feminist reading of Orientalism.* Cambridge University Press.

Weisstein, N. (1993). Psychology constructs the female; or the fantasy life of the male psychologist (with some attention to the fantasies of his friends, the male biologist and the male anthropologist). *Feminism & Psychology,* 3(2), 194–210.

Williams, B., Lewis, T., Manicom, L., & Turley, A. (2025). Systems psychodynamics in social justice movement-building organisations. *Socio-Analysis,* 26(1), v–xiii.

Žižek, S. (1997). *The plague of fantasies.* Verso.

Chapter 3

Superegoic Community

Introduction

At the 1965 Boston Conference on the Education of Psychologists for Community Mental Health – known today as the Swampscott Conference – several clinical psychologists gathered to consider the crisis of relevance facing their discipline. Claiming inspiration from several US-based anti-capitalist struggles of the day (such as the Civil Rights Movement, Second Wave Feminism, and opposition to the Vietnam War), the Swampscott Conference attendees formulated what they called community psychology (Malherbe & Dlamini, 2020). Community psychology, they insisted, would take seriously how individual psychological processes were embedded, formed in, and shaped by the society in which one lived (see Sonn, 2016). Community psychologists would then strive to work with communities, not on them, taking seriously the social justice concerns most pertinent to community members.

The manner by which community psychology was formalised at Swampscott has been criticised for several reasons, including attendees' perfunctory engagements with radical or progressive politics, their refusal to name systems of domination (e.g. capitalism, imperialism, colonialism, patriarchy), their inadequate break from psychology's individualising proclivities, and the lack of attention paid to radical psychological practitioners already working in communities, usually outside of the US (see Gokani & Walsh, 2017; Malherbe & Dlamini, 2020; Montero, 1996). Additionally, almost every conference attendee was a white man from a clinical psychology background (Tebes, 2016).

Despite these criticisms, many of which still apply to community psychologists working today, Swampscott does not, nor did it ever, speak for all of community psychology (Stevens, 2007). Throughout the world, there have always been psychological practitioners working in and with communities to consolidate anti-capitalist resistance. Many of these practitioners, it should be said, do not think of themselves as "community psychologists", and they may well disidentify with the regressive and liberal impulses that mark mainstream community psychology, such as its embrace of corporatised

DOI: 10.4324/9781003612728-3

models of community development, its alignment with nongovernmental organisations committed to global capital, and the part it has played in psychologising and demobilising social movements (Coimbra et al., 2012; Fourie & Terre Blanche, 2019). Nonetheless, I believe that work of this kind does represent a particular kind of community psychology, one that takes place on the liberation psychology paradigm and thus has more invested in anti-capitalist commitments than disciplinary fidelity. Indeed, as noted in Chapter 1, community psychology has taken to the liberation psychology paradigm more enthusiastically than most other formalised psychological fields (Montero et al., 2017).

How then has community psychology – mainstream and otherwise – engaged with the notion of community? Certainly, the variable character of community makes conceptualising it a rather tricky task (Sonn, 2016). Whether they be ideological, value-driven, geographic, or political, communities change all the time, while also retaining identifiable characteristics (Williams, 1975). Much mainstream community psychology has fallen into the trap of attempting to delineate a community's static or unchanging coordinates so that we might better know what a community fundamentally is (Coimbra et al., 2012; Dutta, 2018; Malherbe, 2022). This is not accidental. It speaks to the ways by which the discipline has collaborated with dominant powers that seek to 'know' communities so that they might exercise control and domination over them (Dutta, 2021). Although critical community psychology operating on the liberation psychology paradigm has sought to trouble how community has been taken up by community psychologists (see e.g. Butchart & Seedat, 1990; Coimbra et al., 2012; Dutta, 2018, 2021; Evans et al., 2017; Heller, 1989; Kloos et al., 2012; Sonn, 2016; Malherbe & Cornell, 2022; Mannarini & Salvatore, 2019), more work is required that links community to collectively constituted projects of anti-capitalist emancipation.

Psychoanalysis, despite its usefulness in theorising unstable, contradictory concepts like community (see Tomšič, 2015a), remains largely absent in community psychology's engagements with and formulations of community (Caputo & Tomai, 2020). Lacan's (1998) re-reading of the Freudian superego is, I believe, an especially useful means of bringing a conceptually nuanced – and, importantly, a politicised – notion of community into community psychology praxes situated on the liberation psychology paradigm. Lacan broke from Freud in that he did not understand the superego as an unspoken demand to obey an omnipotent paternal figure and/or a set of cultural mores (McGowan, 2019). Rather, for Lacan (1998), the superego commands subjects to transgress the Law (i.e. the principles underlying social relations) in accordance with capitalist logic. Lacan's superego, in other words, is one that repeatedly demands transgression, or an obscene enjoyment of capitalism that can only be obtained through excess, unrestrained consumption, imperialist antipathy towards the Other[1], and brutally individualised competition (see Tomšič, 2015a). The Lacanian superego, I argue, affords critical community psychologists a useful means of understanding how the unconscious operates to form communities whose seeming dissidence enables them to cohere with capitalism's symbolic structure all the more powerfully. When we consider the Lacanian superegoic community, the ethical task of a critical community psychology (or rather, psychoanalytic liberation psychology) becomes one of assisting activists to construct what I call political communities. Although political communities undoubtedly require transgression, unlike superegoic communities, these transgressions cohere around a shared set of collectively constituted political commitments, rather than capitalism's symbolic order.

In what follows, I examine some of the ways by which community psychology and psychoanalysis have conceptualised community and the problems therein. I then outline Lacan's conception of the superegoic community, which I contrast with the political community. Following this, I draw from my own work to demonstrate how a political community in South Africa intervened in and ultimately refused the superegoic command. I conclude by reflecting on what the political community and the superegoic community mean for how community psychologists understand and engage with the concept of community in ways that break from some of the politically regressive tendencies exemplified by much of their discipline. As such, I consider what it might mean for community psychologists to embrace psychoanalytic liberation psychology.

Community Psychology, Psychoanalysis, and the Problem of Community

Although community psychologists have never insisted on a singular definition of community, within much of community psychology, the concept of community remains bound up with positivism (Sonn et al., 2024). What this means is that for much community psychology, community tends to be drawn on to fix and separate the ontologies and epistemic capacities of community psychologists and the community members with whom they work (Sonn, 2016). Community thus remains a coherent (if also multi-level) object of inquiry that can be known or defined in ways that separate it absolutely from the community psychologist (Coimbra et al., 2012; Dutta, 2018). This separation, Dutta (2021) argues, is not innocent. It reflects colonial capital's dehumanising epistemological project that seeks to determine where legitimate knowledge can be produced and where it cannot, and thus also which lives matter and which do not (see also Ndlovu-Gatsheni, 2018).

Dominant powers can naturalise perceptions of community through definitions of what appear to be irrefutable community characteristics (Evans et al., 2017). Determining good communities from bad, for example, facilitates the exercise of control over communities, that is, the distinction between (good) communities that behave 'correctly' and in accordance with the requirements of an exploitative capitalist order, and (bad) communities that do not (see Coimbra et al., 2012; Sonn et al., 2024). The 'bad' community is often an othered, ghettoised space that represents unsurpassable disadvantage, hierarchical social ordering, dispossession, brokenness, and pain – much of which can be leveraged by those in power to justify the separate development of marginalised, often racialised, communities (see Butchart & Seedat, 1990; Dutta, 2018; Evans et al., 2017). On the other hand, the apparent 'good' community emerges as the embodiment of consensus, connectedness, and peace, with little critical consideration of the normative practices which take place in this community (Malherbe & Cornell, 2022; Williams, 1975). That 'good' communities usually depend on the underdevelopment of 'bad' communities is rarely foregrounded in community psychology (Malherbe, 2022). Fanon (1986 [1967], p. 183) wrote that the obsession of colonial authorities with taxonomising the world into motionless, puritanical categories represents a "Manichean delirium" that prioritises an essentialised ontology over politics. Mainstream community psychology's unspoken designation of communities into moralistic categories ('good' or 'bad') represents a delirium of this kind.

Kloos et al. (2012) note that community psychologists tend to understand community as a locality (i.e. a geographic area) or in terms of relationality (i. e. shared interpersonal relations). These two (often rather static) understandings of community are not necessarily mutually exclusive, evidenced by community psychology's abiding concern with "psychological sense of community", an influential concept developed by Sarason (1974). Psychological sense of community refers to the relational and contextually embedded experiences that occur within a particular locality. It speaks to people's willingness to enter into interdependent relations with one another (McMillan & Chavis, 1986), as well as what erodes dependable social structures and feelings of belonging (Sonn et al., 2024). Although useful in some respects, the term psychological sense of community does not necessarily capture the fact that a community is always remade and reconfigured in the face of broader capitalist structures of power (see Dutta, 2021). As such, community psychologists' engagements with psychological sense of community often reveal the discipline's inclination to definitively know communities for purposes of management and control (see Coimbra et al., 2012). McMillan and Chavis (1986) appear to openly admit this when they proclaim that a psychological sense of community is especially pertinent for those in power seeking to intervene in community life (a life that, it is implied, is to remain necessarily separate from those in power). Understanding communities in terms of a psychological sense of community tends to overlook those community actors who do not fit within this conceptual frame, those who challenge it, or those who undermine it – consciously or unconsciously (Dutta, 2021). Although Sarason (1974) notes that "[a] community has changed, is changing, and will change again" (p. 131), his conception of a psychological sense of community appears, for the most part, unable to adequately accommodate this important insight.

It should be noted that static notions of community do not, in every instance, represent the nucleus around which community psychology orbits. There is often a tension between community psychologists who favour community (i.e. unity and coherence) and those who favour diversity (i.e. a celebration of difference) (see Neal & Neal, 2014). There have, however, been several attempts to disrupt the binary opposition between diversity and community (see Rochira, 2018; Stivala et al., 2016). Mannarini and Salvatore (2019), for example, note that community and diversity should not be understood as antithetical concepts. Instead, each of these concepts is dialectically entangled with the other. 'Community' thus encapsulates community relations founded on difference – a "community of others" (Mannarini & Salvatore, 2019, p. 30). It is, in this sense, possible to build community in ways that encourage diversity (Malherbe & Cornell, 2022). Work of this kind strikes a difficult balance between retaining a community's definitional fluidity and ensuring that diversity does not collapse into a liberalised multicultural tolerance that embraces difference only insofar as it aligns with a broader system of capitalist oppression (Malherbe & Dlamini, 2020); where no difference is more cherished than class difference (Wood, 2007).

Challenging how so much of community psychology has sought to definitively know and rigidly categorise communities requires anti-capitalist community practitioners to look beyond conventional community psychology practice and towards the complex and insurgent ways by which communities seek to 'know' themselves. Communities throughout Rojava, South Africa, Kurdistan, Mexico, Palestine, El Salvador, China, and many others have demonstrated what a fluid, self-determining, and defiant community might look like. These communities identify and are identified in certain ways, but they also push back against oppressive forces that seek to fix their definitional coordinates in alignment with colonial capitalism's imperial mandate. Such insurgent definitions of community are perhaps best understood as what Williams (1975) refers to as knowable communities. Although knowable communities are identifiable in several respects, the arbitrariness of these identifications is continually emphasised and contested (i.e. they are knowable rather than known), and thus how a particular community is identified can be made and remade by collective anti-capitalist struggle. While knowable communities take people's meaning-making practices seriously, these communities hold these practices accountable to a broader set of political commitments. Thus, the knowability of the knowable community is contingent, always subject to the political will of the demos. As such, knowable communities allow for a "re-envisioning of epistemic parameters that simultaneously disrupt and offer alternatives to essentialist notions of community" (Dutta, 2018, p. 275).

Community psychology need not abandon its various conceptions of community (e.g. psychological sense of community; locality; relationality; diversity). Instead, anti-capitalists should work to unmoor these conceptions from the will to know a community absolutely by embracing the contingency of the knowable community. This is, of course, a challenging task that requires rejecting moralisation and binary logic while, at the same time, remaining attentive to how conceptions of community can be mobilised to advance the kinds of critical solidarity needed to consolidate anti-capitalist resistance. As noted earlier, while community psychology interventions situated on the liberation psychology paradigm have taken up this task of troubling rigid conceptions of community (Malherbe & Dlamini, 2020), the psychoanalytic notion of the unconscious[2] remains largely – but not entirely – neglected within this work. As such, we might consider what it is that community psychologists who are committed to troubling and politicising community can learn and have learned from psychoanalysis, which is to say, how community psychologists might embrace psychoanalytic liberation psychology to conceptualise community in a critical manner.

It is in line with a broader trend of erasing the history of psychoanalysis from psychology (see Parker, 2007) that efforts to hold psychoanalysis together with community psychology are largely overlooked, particularly by psychological professionals. Certainly, we have seen a number of community psychologists adopting psychoanalytic theories of community (see e.g. Borg, 2010; Gibson & Swartz, 2008; King & Shelley, 2008; Long, 2002; Malherbe & Cornell, 2022). Psychodynamic and psychotherapeutic theories, in particular, have been taken up by several community psychologists. Some have even suggested that psychoanalysis could serve as useful for guiding the supervision training of community psychology researchers (e.g. Emmite, 1980), although this proposal has not been met with much enthusiasm. There is also a growing knowledge ecology (e.g. training programmes, journal sections, and consortia) on what has been called "community psychoanalysis" (see e.g. Bruns & Barron, 2022; Clarke et al., 2006; Roehrle & Strouse, 2019). In short, although psychoanalysis remains on the margins of community psychology (Caputo & Tomai, 2020), especially with respect to how community psychologists conceptualise community (see King & Shelley, 2008), psychoanalysis has not been rejected outright by all community psychologists.

The marginalisation of psychoanalysis within most of community psychology is somewhat peculiar when we consider that psychoanalysis has always had much to say about community.[3] In his work on group psychology (or *massenpsychologie*), Freud (1921) wrote about the libidinal organisation and unconscious processes at work within collectives, or what he sometimes called (rather disparagingly) "the mass". Through a shared libidinal investment in a group leader, Freud argued, people forged libidinal bonds among themselves, often disparaging those outside of these bonds. Freud's work on group psychology has been especially influential in psychoanalytic scholarship explicitly concerned with community, including, for instance, the work undertaken by Wilfred Bion, the A. K. Rice Institute, and the Tavistock Institute (Rustin & Armstrong, 2019). However, even in therapeutic settings, psychoanalysts have tended to understand the clinic as a point at which different communities (past and present; real and imagined; familial and chosen) converge and reconstitute themselves (Bruns & Barron, 2022). Certainly, Freud's free psychoanalytic clinics mentioned in Chapter 1, as well as the so-called 'social clinics' that followed these, might be read as attempts on the part of psychoanalysts to engage critically with issues of community (see ffytche et al., 2022).

From their systematic review of psychodynamic theories in community psychology, Caputo and Tomai (2020) conclude that for most psychoanalysts, community is a complex object that, rather than forming the sum of community actors, represents a constant interplay of individual components, and thus represents a series of ever-shifting tensions, power differentials, and opposing forces. This does not mean that a community cannot signify anything stable. The psychoanalytic conception of community, Caputo and Tomai (2020) insist, understands communities as governed by rules, repetition, and meaning, all of which shift with the tides of history. As such, contestations over what a community means, or the identifications that it offers, determine the possibilities for cohesion and belonging within a community (see Laclau, 1995).

Psychoanalysis posits that a community can offer subjects identifications that promise to (but cannot ever completely) overcome unconscious anxiety (see Stavrakakis, 2007). Such identifications are significant because they need not be recognised by broader society. In fact, the identifications made available by a community are often psychically appealing precisely because they account for the values, politics, and meanings that broader society represses. A community's identifications are in this way indicative of the dialectic between our conscious wishes for social change – the better life – and our unconscious impulses to repeat (see Caputo & Tomai, 2020). Psychoanalysis, in short, offers us a notion of community that straddles the subjective and the objective, which is to say, conscious knowledge of the self, others, society, and experience, and the unconscious disruption of such knowledge – both of which are mediated by material reality.

In recent years, Koh and Twemlow have, over a series of papers, begun the work of systematically conceptualising community from a psychoanalytic perspective (see Koh & Twemlow, 2016a, 2016b; Koh & Twemlow, 2017; Koh & Twemlow, 2018). They insist that because a community is both a subjective and an objective entity, psychoanalytic theory can assist us in understanding the dynamic qualities of a community, including the individual and collective experiences of community (Koh & Twemlow, 2016a). They posit the following:

[A community] emphasizes the unconscious, collective, psychological tasks involved in creating and sustaining a community, as well as those tasks involved in it achieving its reason for being. The core psychological tasks are those concerned with the creation of bonding among a community's membership and formation of its boundary and identity. Each of these psychological tasks is underpinned by unconscious psychic processes.

(Koh & Twemlow, 2017, p. 270)

Koh and Twemlow (2016b) outline ten principles that undergird their psychoanalytic formulation of community: (1) the unconscious facets of community life; (2) the social interactions, common interests, and shared symbolic systems forged through unconscious processes; (3) the group dynamics – large and small – which make up community life, all of which are in flux, and which connect to acknowledged and unacknowledged trauma; (4) the identifications which bind individuals within a community; (5) the abstract or symbolic qualities of a community; (6) the symbolic functions of a community which are determined by individual subjects; (7) the role of intersubjective experiences in forming community; (8) how symbolisation, or making sense of experience, forms community; (9) the ways people benefit from a community and how a community influences internalisation; and finally (10) the ways by which a community can be assessed in relation to its ability to facilitate a subject's capacity to relate and (re)produce. The effectiveness with which a community embodies these principles, Koh and Twemlow (2018) propose, depends on its capacity to facilitate how people process tension and conflict, defend against anxiety, and adapt to challenges.

While expansive, psychoanalytic work on community, as well as community psychology work that draws on psychoanalytic thought to understand community, has tended to neglect the superego. This is unfortunate given the political insights that conceptions of the superego can afford to us. Therefore, it is to the superegoic community that we must now turn, after which we will consider how knowable communities can combat the politically regressive tendencies of the superegoic community.

Capitalism and the Superegoic Community

The superego, like several other psychoanalytic concepts (e.g. ego, the unconscious, narcissism, the 'Freudian slip'), has entered into popular parlance, and is therefore not a wholly unfamiliar term to many people. Indeed, the superego is often evoked to refer to a vague sense of personal morality or an external ethical code. This is not quite what Freud meant by the term. He spoke of the superego as a kind of authority – one that is both socio-cultural and parental – that supplants itself in the psyche (Freud, 1924). Nothing is hidden from the Freudian superego, not even our thoughts. The superego is always judging the ego against an impossible ego ideal (Freud, 1930). Our striving towards this ideal is what structures our desire. Therefore, for Freud, the superego denotes a libidinal authority whose judgement over us results in anxiety and determines our psychic drives (McGowan, 2013). The superego, in other words, speaks to a radical otherness that exists both within and outside of us (Barnard-Naudé, 2023), one that is always bearing down cruelly on the ego (Copjec, 1989).

What does the superego mean for community? Freud (1921) theorised that people, when in group settings, turn their superego judgements over to a leader, subsequently internalising the leader's commands (importantly, Freud noted that a ruling idea could function in the place of a leader). By obeying the leader's commands, the individual subject is afforded a sense of security and belonging, and in this regard, the superego psychically binds subjects into a community. At the same time, the sense of belonging afforded by the Freudian superegoic community is usually premised on hostility towards an outgroup which is said to pose a threat to the kinds of psychic security afforded by one's own superegoic community. The superegoic community, in this sense, attempts to secure its identity by insisting on what it is not, which is also what it opposes. Paradoxically, then, the self-identification of the superegoic community depends on the communities it opposes.

The Freudian superegoic community, while certainly finding some resonance in our contemporary capitalist conjuncture (the global rise of right-wing populism and neo-fascism come to mind here), should nonetheless be understood against Freud's particular cultural, social, and historical milieu. As Tomšič (2015b) explains, the industrial capitalism of mid-nineteenth- and mid-twentieth-century Europe (forged through war and colonial expansion) in which Freud lived ushered in a culture of prohibition. This meant that the Freudian superegoic community required subjects to give up, postpone, repress, or lose something in accordance with their duty to a social and/or political authority (see Stavrakakis, 2007). The neoliberal capitalism of today, however, functions quite differently. Our epoch is characterised by consumption, perpetual growth, increasing colonial occupation, dispossession, genocide, and ever-expanding exchange value (see Ndlovu-Gatsheni, 2018; Tomšič, 2015a, 2015b). It is within a context marked by changing capitalist relations that Lacan (1998) undertook his re-reading of the Freudian superego.

For Lacan, the superego commands of the subject what he called jouissance, or enjoyment, which – as we saw in Chapter 2 – refers to an unconscious investment of pleasure into the sorts of displeasure that come from not quite fitting in with a prevailing order (Stavrakakis, 2007). Enjoyment, Lacan posited, is closely tied with the excessive demands of capitalist accumulation (Gherovici, 2018), demands rooted in imperialist, ecological, and patriarchal violence (see Chapter 1). Therefore, we do not enjoy spontaneously (Žižek, 2022). Our enjoyment forms part of a psychic injunction to transgress within the bounds set by capital. The superego of today's capitalism commands that we enjoy transgressing the social limit – or the principles underlying our social relations – in line with the consumptive imperial logic underwriting contemporary regimes of capital accumulation. Put differently, we could say that contemporary capitalism manages our enjoyment by demanding that we enjoy excessively (Soler, 2014). It should be emphasised that the superego, for Lacan, is defined by its unrelenting command to enjoy rather than the attainment of enjoyment. Indeed, the enjoyment that the superego promises is non-existent precisely because it is always prohibited by the Law (Žižek, 1994). The Law can therefore be understood as the viciously sadistic source of the superego (Copjec, 1998). In short, Lacan makes clear that the superego no longer commands in accordance with prohibition, but in accordance with unrestrained capitalist excess. The superegoic community is, in turn, formed among those committed to the superego's command to enjoy excessively.

The Lacanian superego is unrelenting. It mocks the subject's inevitable failure to meet its impossible demands while the subject, consequently, experiences an increasing sense of guilt that stems from repressing their condemned strivings to meet the superegoic command (Žižek, 2022). Therefore, the more we give in to the superego's commands, the more it asks of us (McGowan, 2019). The continual pressure to transgress that which the superego commands (a pressure sustained by the libidinal energy of the id; Žižek, 2022) mirrors the continually deferred satisfaction promised – but never delivered – by capitalism (e.g. the apparent satisfaction of working harder, consuming more, producing better, eviscerating supposed competition or threats to livelihood). The superegoic command to enjoy, we might say, cedes our enjoyment to an unending capitalistic demand to enjoy (Soler, 2014); with the true injunction of the superego being to enjoy our suffering and, ultimately, to enjoy our capitalism (Tomšič, 2015a).

Although the Law being transgressed through the superegoic command may be unjust, this is not why the superego commands transgression of the Law. It is simply transgression for transgression's sake. In other words, the superego does not command that we transgress capitalist Law to challenge or dismantle this Law, but rather to reinscribe desire under capitalism in seemingly subversive ways. Genuine desire is thus dissolved into the network of pseudo-satisfactions offered by capitalism (Jameson, 1974). It is in this sense that the superegoic command to enjoy appropriates our dissident unconscious energies, ensuring that we transgress social relations in accordance with capitalism's logic of excess (McGowan, 2019), thus securing our libidinal investment in capitalism (see Žižek, 2022). The superego cannot represent an ethical or emancipatory force because of its entwinement with capitalism. It can only produce unreflective, guilty subjects envious of the state of full enjoyment that they imagine the Other to have attained and from which they imagine they have been excluded. These subjects are bound together by a shared paranoia of the Other's enjoyment. In this regard, "the sadistic threats of the superego arise from a prior sense of *being threatened*" (Barnard-Naudé, 2023, p. 35). The superegoic community, therefore, resists any sort of collectively constituted ethos precisely because it is a community that positions the Other as preventing or stealing the enjoyment that was promised to community insiders (Žižek, 1994, 2022). As per the dictates of racial and patriarchal capitalism, the Other usually refers to those most marginalised, who hold the least power in capitalism's social order.

The Lacanian superego produces a paradoxical kind of community. Where the community of the Freudian superego invests libidinal power in the leader and thus the political project represented by this leader, the Lacanian superego invests libidinal power in the logic of capital. As such, the libido turns inwards to produce "an extreme, selfish, narcissistic individualism. The leader is no longer an authoritarian father figure, but a mirror in which the hyper-alienated, sociopathic, self-obsessed consumer-spectators of an atomised social order see themselves" (Faulkner, 2021, p. 57). Put differently, community is created through the subject's adherence to a capitalist subjectivity that commands enjoyment of capitalist excess (related to excessive production and consumption, as well as excessive hatred along racialised, classed, gendered, and ecological lines) and a commitment to private property (Malherbe, 2024). Transgression of the Law can, therefore, only assume forms that are approved by the (fundamentally capitalist) superegoic community. In this, Žižek (1994) posits that the guilt of transgressing the Law, or rather the fetishistic disavowal of guilt, creates among those within the superegoic community a solidarity-in-guilt, which serves as the structuring principle for the psychic binds that make up this community.

It is because the excessive capitalistic enjoyment for which the subject strives when obeying the superego's command is never spoken that the superego operates on the level of the unconscious, functioning covertly and thus all the more effectively (Žižek, 1994). As such, we cannot do away with or entirely eradicate the superego because we cannot completely 'settle the score' with our unconscious (Soler, 2014). Attempts to eliminate, ignore, or repress the superego are likely to prolong internal conflicts within ourselves (Copjec, 1989). We can, however, assume some distance from the superegoic community; living in "productive tension" with it (Barnard-Naudé, 2023, p. 32) and speaking its commands in order to weaken the psychic grip it holds over us (McGowan, 2019). Although the superego commands that communities enjoy in accordance with capitalist excess, we can also attain enjoyment from constituent sacrifice (McGowan, 2013); from missing the absent cause of our desires and committing to political causes that exceed individual enjoyment (Žižek, 2022). The sacrifices required by an anti-capitalist political cause (e.g. sacrificing time, resources, energy, security, and/or the mythic solace of capitalist identifications) can move the subject to break from libidinal attachments to the superegoic command.

Consolidating the Political Community

Dutta has considered how community psychologists situated in the decolonial turn might think of community in political terms. She writes:

> [D]ecoloniality demands a radical transformation in how we think about community in community psychology – namely, abandoning notions of community as phenomenon of interest or site of inquiry/intervention to focus instead on a radical relationality capable of dismantling or rendering extraneous colonial patterns of power and relationality [and to] reclaim community as political, as resistance, in contrast to essentialist (biological, cultural, or sociological) conceptions of community, while underscoring the criticality of lived engagement with struggles.
>
> (Dutta, 2021, p. 61)

Our dissident psychic energies (i.e. our unconscious drive to undermine and transgress) need not necessarily be appropriated by the superegoic community. These energies can also be harnessed by political communities that create psychic binds through a shared commitment to a radically democratic political programme, commitments that undoubtedly require sacrifice. To resist the superegoic command by reconstituting 'community' as a fundamentally political signifier is, of course, not to do away with the imperative to transgress the Law. However, when transgression forms part of a political community, it is not transgression for the sake of it. It is, instead, to transgress in the service of anti-capitalism. Committing to a political community thus allows us to take a position relative to the superego and to determine our desires in accordance with a political project predicated on emancipatory solidarity rather than capitalist solidarity-in-guilt.

Glynos (2001, p. 103) offers some provocative, though rather non-prescriptive, remarks which pertain to how we might think psychoanalytically about the political community:

> [W]hat kind of *community* is (even theoretically) possible for subjects of the drive? What insights can Lacanian clinical theory offer us? Since a Lacanian conception of community eschews ideas of shared values or common symbolic identifications; and since it suggests that our social bond should also not be based on a common fantasmatic transgression (which makes possible a community of subjects of desire), what other ways are there of thinking a community of subjects? Indeed, is a *social* subject of the drive possible?

Glynos seems to point to the need to hold the political community to a radical kind of openness that builds anti-capitalist commitments through what Mouffe (2005) calls conflictual consensus – an ongoing process of collectively constituted deliberation. As such, we make, strengthen, and connect anti-capitalist political communities with and through agonistic engagements and conflict. The political community, therefore, does not assume a definitive or unchanging formation. It resists capitalism's psychotic foreclosures, neurotic repressions, and delusional claims of mastery.

The political community constantly makes and remakes itself through collective, yet agonistically conceived, anti-capitalist fantasies of emancipation. When we understand emancipation not as a fixed or idealised point of arrival, but as a state of desire that is always undergoing collective determinations, then sacrifice to the anti-capitalist collective – rather than to capitalist projections of excess – becomes part and parcel of how subjectivity is made within the political community. Those who compromise the political community compose themselves through their lack of mastery, and in this can derive enjoyment through sacrifice (Stavrakakis, 2007). To enjoy subjective lack within the political community is to loose subjectivity from the superegoic obligation to enjoy excessively (Žižek, 2022).

The political community, we might say, resembles Williams's (1975) conception of the knowable community (i.e. an identifiable rather than wholly identified community). The knowable community, unlike the known community, does not use knowledge to stabilise a singularly defined Truth (Newman, 2004). Rather, the knowable political community is constituted by commitments to an anti-capitalist cause, commitments that are repeatedly reformulated, rather than predetermined or eternally known, through conflictual consensus, debate, and sacrifice. Knowledge is thus made and refined in and for collective anti-capitalist struggle, moving in accordance with the emancipatory requirements of this struggle.

Community psychologists should not understand the political community as entirely unwilling to fix meaning. Meaning is, after all, important in the consolidation of political communities, even if, within the political community, meaning is also contingent. As Laclau (1995) puts it, meaning is both impossible (it cannot be determined with any finality) and necessary (it is a requirement for driving anti-capitalist politics). If meaning within knowable political communities is fixed, it is a fixity that is knowingly partial and always open to the radically democratic demands of the anti-capitalist collective.

It is because political communities are made through intense organisation, longstanding bonds, and complex networks of solidarity that they have proven very difficult to sustain, especially in contexts where meeting the basic means of survival is tremendously difficult. Political communities should also not be fetishised. There may well be regressive instances (e.g. racism, sexism, xenophobia, heteronormativity) that undermine political communities. Moreover, political communities are not immune to capitalist co-optation. Many formerly anti-capitalist political communities have been subsumed into capital's ideological apparatuses. Thus, the anti-capitalism through which political communities are forged must be continually defended, nurtured, and made to encompass all struggles for liberation if, indeed, these communities are to last.

The political community does not seek to answer to the riddle of human history in the way that Marx (1978 [1844]) believed the arrival of communism would. Instead, by traversing collectively constituted visions of emancipation, the political community draws from people's dissident psychic energies to advance anti-capitalist emancipation. In this, the political community carries within it a degree of psychic appeal that is fundamental to its consolidation.

Case Reflection

Engaging with the superegoic community and – even more importantly – consolidating political communities represent significant yet almost completely neglected ways by which community psychologists can break from static conceptions of community. Turning away from the superegoic community by working with activists to consolidate knowable political communities represents a genuinely psycho-political project, one that is alive to the materiality of domination as well as the unconscious forces upon which capitalist powers so often rely. It is also a project that moves community psychology towards psychoanalytic liberation psychology.

In what follows, I reflect on my own community-engaged work in the south of Johannesburg. Before moving on to this reflection though, it should be noted that in South Africa, the superego has always functioned in relation to the particular era of capital accumulation in which it is embedded. Thus, the continuities of South Africa's history live within the constitution of today's superegoic functioning. Colonial and apartheid-era superegos have not been buried entirely (Barnard-Naudé, 2023). Both form part of how the superego functions in South Africa's contemporary racial capitalist order. And of course, the superego has never held the same degree of influence over every subject living in South Africa. There have always been those who resist the superegoic command.

Turning to the case reflection: in 2015, socialist movement activists in Johannesburg initiated a series of protests and demonstrations. They were demanding that the South African state provide basic public services (e.g. sanitation, parks, housing, improved roads, clean running water, electricity) in their community. It was during these protests that several protesters and, it is believed, others who were not affiliated with the protests began to steal from and even destroy some of the homes and small businesses belonging to foreign nationals living in the community. Several foreign nationals were also physically assaulted during this time. Those enacting this xenophobic violence were able to pursue the capitalist logic of individualistic accumulation through transgression. These transgressions differed fundamentally from the modes of politically dissident transgressions carried out by the protesters.

Indeed, the transgressions enacted by the protests were put into the service of a broader socialist agenda, rather than a command to *enjoy capitalism* (see Tomšič, 2015a).

Of course, those engaging in xenophobic violence did not occupy a dominant societal position. They were, themselves, living in conditions of grinding poverty. Stealing from the stores owned by foreign nationals was certainly, to some degree, driven by material need. However, it remains the case that wealthier individuals from surrounding communities were not targeted during this time. Moreover, stealing from foreign nationals took place in conjunction with assaults on foreign nationals, which points towards the ideological – rather than the purely opportunistic – character of the xenophobia. The common struggles faced by those comprising the xenophobic superegoic community and foreign nationals were obscured by the superego's hyper-individualised command to enjoy capitalist excess. In this instance, excess did not mean excessive consumption, but rather the excessively violent structures upon which capitalist accumulation depends.

Despite the political traction that the movement was gaining with respect to achieving its goals through the protests, the movement leaders immediately deferred all protest action once they had been made aware of the xenophobic violence taking place in the community. Following the suspension of the protests, movement actors worked with foreign nationals to ensure that that which had been stolen from them was returned. Later, movement activists collaborated with foreign nationals to host a series of community events which aimed to promote cohesion and solidarity within the community. It was only after the safety of foreign nationals in the community was guaranteed that the movement resumed its protest activities.

Incorporating the struggles of foreign nationals into the social movement's political purview altered not only how the movement undertook political action, but also expanded the emancipatory fantasies ungirding this action. Fantasies of emancipation were emboldened and rendered more ambitious by attending to and making connections between a multitude of struggles against racial capitalism. Like we saw in Chapter 2, the emancipatory fantasy frame accrued strength from an expansive anti-capitalist struggle, one that encompassed a variety of intersectional concerns. In this regard, the movement did not offer coherent or definitive identifications to those aligning with its anti-capitalist programme. Instead, movement actors sought to facilitate a space within which people could negotiate – and collectively agonise over – how they would action their fantasies of emancipation (see Malherbe & Cornell, 2022). It was within this political community that fantasies of liberation were shaped by and held accountable to the struggling collective, thereby reconstituting the political through the human (see Ndlovu-Gatsheni, 2018).

The xenophobia exhibited in the community at this time is not anomalous in South Africa. Poor foreign nationals living in the country regularly incur blame for centuries of colonial devastation as well as the inequalities engendered by the racial capitalist order to which the present-day South African state is committed (Kerr et al., 2019). Several prominent politicians and news media personnel have, over the years, perpetuated such divisive xenophobic sentiments precisely because it absolves them of responsibility for taking action against a system that secures their class position (Neocosmos, 2008). Like other incidents of xenophobic violence in South Africa, those occurring at the time of the 2015 protests received considerable coverage in the South African media, often in an attempt to delegitimise the protests. Yet, the manner by which the social movement actors intervened in these xenophobic attacks, taking direct action to stop them, received virtually no media coverage. This kind of neglect on the part of the South African media is a commonplace strategy of making state-led, often brutally violent, police interventions appear legitimate.

Some time after the protests, several colleagues and I worked with movement activists, foreign nationals, and others in the community to produce a participatory documentary film (this was not the same documentary film, nor the same community, that appeared in Chapter 2's case reflection). Much of this film focused on the history of the movement and its struggles. Inclusive of this history were the movement's anti-xenophobic interventions. Showcasing these interventions was an important counter to the mainstream media's preoccupation with depicting xenophobia in the community without considering how xenophobia was being combated within the community, by the community. At a series of public screenings of the film (e.g. in community halls, at community events, and in several commercial districts throughout Johannesburg), activists presented their political work, anti-capitalist projects, and underlying fantasies of liberation to different audiences. Activists at the screening events also engaged with broader organisational work, reflecting on which strategies and tactics had worked, which had not, where and how future protests would be conducted, and which struggles were most urgent. It was at these public screenings that movement activists fostered avenues of solidarity with workers, community members, and other activists facing similar struggles who were committed to a comparable (although not identical) anti-capitalist programme.

It may be argued that the xenophobic superegoic community operating at the time of the protests offered a sacrifice of sorts (e.g. the sacrifice of good standing in the community). However, such a sacrifice was always held accountable to the superegoic command to enjoy in excess. In other words, the superegoic community moved through sacrifice in order to enjoy excessively. This was not the case with the social movement's anti-xenophobic actions, whereby sacrifice was held accountable to its anti-capitalist commitments – a sacrifice in service of an emancipatory cause. Accordingly, at public screenings of the documentary, the social movement, as a political community, structured enjoyment by appealing to the kinds of sacrifices, fantasies of liberation, and commitments required to advance anti-capitalist struggle, rather than a command to enjoy excessively *a la* the xenophobic superegoic community.

Many of the screening events were marked with intense affect and dis-agreement, as well as feelings of disappointment and despair at what it meant to undertake struggles in such trying economic conditions. Colleagues and I were invited by community members to assist with facilitating some of these public screenings, to hold space to express affect and to work with audiences to surface underlying agonism, and to attempt to incorporate this agonism into the political community – sitting in it and reflecting on it to consider what it tells us about waging community-led anti-capitalist struggle. Audience members, for instance, disagreed on the role of the state in their struggles; how anti-capitalist movements could connect with community initiatives that were delinking from capitalist production (e.g. worker cooperatives and organic subsistence farming); and how leadership structures should be composed within the movement. The point here was not to resolve these dis-agreements, but to propel the movement through them; to allow anti-capitalism to assume different formations that emerged in agnostic interaction. In facilitating space to articulate varying (sometimes incompatible) formations, actions, and knowledges through which to compose the movement, the political community was opened up to different desires, strengthening itself through its lack of mastery.

Importantly, the movement screened the documentary film at several political meetings to which my colleagues and I were not invited. The consolidation of the political community may very well be hindered by psychology (and its assumptions of mastery) or the presence of psychologists (see Parker, 2011). As recounted in Chapter 1, central to psychoanalytic liberation psychology is the ceding of disciplinary hubris, which is to say, knowing when anti-capitalist struggle does not have any use for the psy-disciplines. The point to be made here is to remain in dialogue with activists so that we are aware of what role, if any, psychological practitioners can play in community-led efforts to consolidate anti-capitalist struggle.

Our psychoanalytic liberation psychology intervention was not concerned with formulating the movement's political community from scratch. The intensive work of movement-building had begun well over twenty years ago in this community. Rather, we sought to work with residents of this political community to advance their anti-capitalist struggles in self-determined ways. To do so, we worked in and with the political community to co-produce a documentary film that communicated its anti-capitalist commitments to new publics. Public screenings of the film then served as sites of political reflection, whereby activists could engage with tensions and agonisms within their movement so as to consolidate the movement through its internal contradictions. This is especially important in places like South Africa, where under-resourced struggles for liberation are repeatedly silenced, repressed, or brutally suppressed. Strengthening the political community (and thus contributing to efforts that turn away from the commands of the superegoic community) must, therefore, always be guided by the emancipatory requirements articulated by political communities themselves.

Conclusion

> Without community there is no liberation, only the most vulnerable and temporary armistice between an individual and her oppression. But community must not mean a shedding of our differences, nor the pathetic pretense that these differences do not exist.
>
> (Lorde, 2017, p. 18)

Formalised community psychology has struggled to break from static conceptions of community (e.g. community as a known geographic locale or community as bound by a fixed and identifiable set of values; Kloos et al., 2012), and has sought to know the community definitively, thereby lending itself to projects that seek to control and manage communities in accordance with capital accumulation (Coimbra et al., 2012; Sonn et al., 2024). Many critical community psychologists, unsatisfied with how community has been mobilised by so many within their discipline, have sought to stretch and expand the notion of community by engaging with it as a complex, ever-shifting site of political interests, affective interactions, and material mediations. In this chapter, I have sought to contribute to this critical community psychology work via the insights of psychoanalytic liberation, drawing from the Lacanian conception of the superego to understand how unconscious mechanisms psychically bind people into a community defined by a mode of transgressive, yet essentially capitalistic, enjoyment. It is against these superegoic communities that community psychologists can work with activist groups to consolidate political communities through which self-determined struggles can find expression and where solidarity can be established via an agonistic process that structures enjoyment through sacrifice and anti-capitalist commitment.

In the *Economic and Philosophical Manuscripts*, Marx (1978 [1844]) argues that individuals are free only when their nature is owed to themselves; when their sources of life, creativity, energy, and reproduction are not determined by or sold to others. Capitalism, Marx argues, produces communities of things rather than communities of people. He was referring here to the material circumstances of labour under capitalism, however, there are surely also psychic affects engendered by these circumstances. These psychic affects should not be ignored by psychological practitioners committed to an intersectional anti-capitalist politics. When we take seriously the superego, we take seriously how the community of things co-opts our unconscious dissident energies to advance a capitalist rationality that is based on excess, hyper-individualisation, and consumption. However, those practising psychoanalytic liberation psychology in communities need to consider not only the kinds of unconscious mechanisms that structure community life. Work of this sort should also strive to make itself of use to political communities that redirect people's dissident psychic energies into the realisation of a humanistic community that breaks from the community of things. Such political communities are, of course, not shorn of unconscious desire, but they can offer us the psychic tools needed to impede the superego's unrelenting command to enjoy capitalist accumulation.

Notes

1 Throughout this chapter, I use "the Other" to refer to those who have been othered through the discursive and ideological mechanisms of a racist, imperialist, and patriarchal capitalist social order that depends on the exploitation and even destruction of the Other's labour, lives, and lands. The Other, we might say, is made into an other through a process of othering which relies in large part on violently divisive rhetoric (e.g. racism, sexism, xenophobia, heteronormativity) that coheres with coloniality's materially violent hierarchicalisation of being (Ndlovu-Gatsheni, 2018). Therefore, I use "the Other" somewhat differently from Lacan, who deployed this term in a rather complex, often quite confusing, manner to refer to an imagined authority figure, that which grounds dialogue, or a structuring order that governs our behaviour (see Žižek, 2022).
2 In classic psychoanalytic theory, the unconscious refers to a kind of force within our thinking that undermines and opposes our supposedly rational wishes (Lear, 2005; see also Chapter 4).
3 It should, however, be noted that psychoanalysis has, for its part, almost completely ignored community psychology. Although this is not always the case, particularly in anti-capitalist psychoanalytic practice (see e.g. Sheehi & Sheehi, 2022).

References

Barnard-Naudé, J. (2023). Burying the superego? *Social Dynamics*, 49(1), 30–48.
Borg, M. B., Jr. (2010). Community psychoanalysis: Developing a model of psychoanalytically-informed community crisis intervention. In N. Lange & M. Wagner (eds), *Community psychology: New directions* (pp. 1–66). Nova Science Publishers.
Bruns, G., & Barron, J. (2022). Psychoanalysis and the community–introductory considerations. *The International Journal of Psychoanalysis*, 103(1), 108–119.
Butchart, A., & Seedat, M. (1990). Within and without: Images of community and implications for South African psychology. *Social Science & Medicine*, 31(10), 1093–1102.
Caputo, A., & Tomai, M. (2020). A systematic review of psychodynamic theories in community psychology: Discovering the unconscious in community work. *Journal of Community Psychology*, 48(6), 2069–2085.
Clarke, S., Hahn, H., Hoggett, P., & Sideris, T. (2006). Psychoanalysis and community. *Psychoanalysis, Culture & Society*, 11(2), 199–216.
Coimbra, J. L., Duckett, P., Fryer, D., Makkawi, I., Menezes, I., Seedat, M., & Walker, C. (2012). Rethinking community psychology: Critical insights. *The Australian Community Psychologist*, 24(2), 135–142.

Copjec, J. (1989). The sartorial superego. *October*, 50, 57–95.

Dutta, U. (2018). Decolonizing "community" in community psychology. *American Journal of Community Psychology*, 62(3–4),272–282.

Dutta, U. (2021). Decentering "community" in community psychology: Towards radical relationality and resistance. In S. Kessi, S. Suffla, & M. Seedat (eds), *Decolonial enactments in community psychology* (pp. 53–72). Springer.

Emmite, P. L. (1980). Psychoanalytic model for training in supervision, research and community development: A personal experience in mexico city. *Journal of Community Psychology*, 8(2), 176–188.

Evans, S. D., Duckett, P., Lawthom, R., & Kivell, N. (2017). Positioning the critical in community psychology. In M. Bond, I. Serrano-Garcia, C. B. Keys, & M. Shinn (eds), *APA handbook of community psychology: Theoretical foundations, core concepts, and emerging challenges* (pp. 107–127). American Psychological Association.

Fanon, F. (1986 [1967]). *Black skin, white masks*. Pluto.

Faulkner, N. (2021). *Alienation, spectacle, and revolution: A critical Marxist essay*. Resistance Books.

ffytche, M., Ryan, J., & Soreanu, R. (2022). Psychoanalysis for the people: Interrogations and innovations. *Psychoanalysis and History*, 24(3), 253–267.

Fourie, E., & Terre Blanche, M. (2019). About accountants and translators: Reshaping community engagement in South African psychology. *South African Journal of Psychology*, 49, 39–51.

Freud, S. (1921). Group psychology and the analysis of the ego. In J. Strachey (ed., trans.), *The standard edition of the complete psychological works of Sigmund Freud, vol. 18*. Hogarth Press.

Freud, S. (1924). Neurosis and psychosis. In J. Strachey (ed., trans.), *The standard edition of the complete psychological works of Sigmund Freud, vol. 19*. Hogarth Press.

Freud, S. (1930). Civilization and its discontents. In J. Strachey (ed., trans.), *The standard edition of the complete psychological works of Sigmund Freud, vol. 21*. Hogarth Press.

Gherovici, P. (2018). Psychoanalysis of poverty, poverty of psychoanalysis. In P. Gherovici & C. Christian (eds), *Psychoanalysis in the barrios: Race, class, and the unconscious* (pp. 221–235). Routledge.

Gibson, K., & Swartz, L. (2008). Putting the 'heart' back into community psychology: Some South African examples. *Psychodynamic Practice*, 14(1), 59–75.

Glynos, J. (2001). 'There is no Other of the Other': Symptoms of a decline in symbolic faith, or, Žižek's anti-capitalism. *Paragraph*, 24(2), 78–110.

Gokani, R., & Walsh, R. T. (2017). On the historical and conceptual foundations of a community psychology of social transformation. *American Journal of Community Psychology*, 59(3–4), 284–294.

Heller, K. (1989). Ethical dilemmas in community intervention. *American Journal of Community Psychology*, 17(3), 367.

Jameson, F. (1974). *Marxism and form: Twentieth-century dialectical theories of literature*. Princeton University Press.

Kerr, P., Durrheim, K., & Dixon, J. (2019). Xenophobic violence and struggle discourse in South Africa. *Journal of Asian and African Studies*, 54(7), 995–1011.

King, R. A., & Shelley, C. A. (2008). Community feeling and social interest: Adlerian parallels, synergy and differences with the field of community psychology. *Journal of Community & Applied Social Psychology*, 18(2), 96–107.

Kloos, B., Hill, J., Thomas E., Wandersman, A., Elias, M. J., & Dalton, J. H. (2012). *Community psychology: Linking individuals and communities* (3rd ed.). Thomson/ Wadsworth.

Koh, E., & Twemlow, S. W. (2016a). Towards a psychoanalytic concept of community (I): Consideration of current concepts. *International Journal of Applied Psychoanalytic Studies*, 13(1), 53–64.

Koh, E., & Twemlow, S. (2016b). Towards a psychoanalytic concept of community (II): Relevant psychoanalytic principles. *International Journal of Applied Psychoanalytic Studies*, 13(2), 124–141.

Koh, E., & Twemlow, S. W. (2017). Towards a psychoanalytic concept of community (III): A proposal. *International Journal of Applied Psychoanalytic Studies*, 14(4), 261–272.

Koh, E., & Twemlow, S. W. (2018). Towards a psychoanalytic concept of community (IV): The well-functioning community. *International Journal of Applied Psychoanalytic Studies*, 15(1), 5–15.

Lacan, J. (1998). *The seminar of Jacques Lacan, Book XX: Encore 1972–1973*. W. W. Norton & Co.

Laclau, E. (1995). *Emancipation(s)*. Verso.

Lear, J. (2005). *Freud*. Routledge.

Long, C. (2002). Psychoanalytic community psychology: Crossing worlds or worlds apart. In L. P. Swartz, K. Gibson, & T. Gelman (eds), *Reflective practice: Psychodynamic ideas in the community* (pp. 113–124). HSRC.

Lorde, A. (2017). *The master's tools will never dismantle the master's house*. Random House.

Malherbe, N. (2022). *For an anti-capitalist psychology of community*. Springer.

Malherbe, N. (2024). Anti-capitalist subjectivity: Considerations of fantasy, (in) action, and solidarity-building. *Subjectivity*, 31(1), 59–78.

Malherbe, N., & Cornell, J. (2022). Considering poststructuralist discursive community psychology. *Social and Personality Psychology Compass*, 16(4), e12661.

Malherbe, N. & Dlamini, S. (2020). Troubling history and diversity: Disciplinary decadence in community psychology. *Community Psychology in Global Perspective*, 6(2/1), 144–157.

Mannarini, T., & Salvatore, S. (2019). Making sense of ourselves and others: A contribution to the community-diversity debate. *Community Psychology in Global Perspective*, 5(1), 26–37.

Marx, K. (1978 [1844]). Economic and philosophical manuscripts. In R. C. Tucker (ed.), *The Marx-Engels reader* (pp. 66–125). Norton.

McGowan, T. (2013). *Enjoying what we don't have: The political project of psychoanalysis*. University of Nebraska Press.

McGowan, T. (2019). Superego and the law. In Y. Stavrakakis (ed.), *Routledge handbook of psychoanalytic political theory* (pp. 139–140). Routledge.

McMillan, D. W. & Chavis, D. M. (1986). Sense of community: Definition and theory. *Journal of Community Psychology*, 14, 6–23.

Montero, M. (1996). Parallel lives: Community psychology in Latin America and the United States. *American Journal of Community Psychology*, 24, 589–605.

Montero, M., Sonn, C. C., & Burton, M. (2017). Community psychology and liberation psychology: A creative synergy for an ethical and transformative praxis. In

M. A. Bond, I. Serrano-García, C. B. Keys, & M. Shinn (eds), *APA handbook of community psychology, vol. 1* (pp. 149–167). American Psychological Association.

Mouffe. C. (2005). *On the political.* Routledge.

Ndlovu-Gatsheni, S. J. (2018). *Epistemic freedom in Africa: Deprovincialization and decolonization.* Routledge.

Neal, Z. P., & Neal, J. W. (2014). The incompatibility of diversity and sense of community. *American Journal of Community Psychology,* 53(1–2), 1–12.

Neocosmos, M. (2008). The politics of fear and the fear of politics: Reflections on xenophobic violence in South Africa. *Journal of Asian and African Studies,* 43(6), 586–594.

Newman, S. (2004). Interrogating the master: Lacan and radical politics. *Psychoanalysis, Culture & Society,* 9(3), 298–314.

Parker, I. (2007). *Revolution in psychology: Alienation to emancipation.* Pluto.

Parker, I. (2011). *Lacanian psychoanalysis: Revolutions in subjectivity.* Routledge.

Rochira, A. (2018). What is the role of sense of community in multiracial societies? A contribution to the community–diversity dialectic: A genetic psychology approach. *Journal of Community Psychology,* 46(8), 972–982.

Roehrle, B., & Strouse, J. (2019). Community psychological perspective of psychotherapy: A contradiction?. *Community Psychology in Global Perspective,* 5(1), 7–25.

Rustin, M., & Armstrong, D. (2019). Psychoanalysis, social science and the Tavistock tradition. *Psychoanalysis, Culture & Society,* 24(4), 473–492.

Sarason, S. B. (1974). *The psychological sense of community: Prospects for a community psychology.* Jossey-Bass.

Sheehi, L., & Sheehi, S. (2022). *Psychoanalysis under occupation: Practicing resistance in Palestine.* Routledge.

Soler, C. (2014). *Lacan - the unconscious reinvented.* Routledge.

Sonn, C. C. (2016). Swampscott in international context: Expanding our ecology of knowledge. *American Journal of Community Psychology,* 58, 309–313.

Sonn, C. C., Fernández, J. S., MouraJr., J. F., Madyaningrum, M. E., & Malherbe, N. (2024). Decolonisation in and beyond community psychologies: A transnational plurilogue. In C. C. Sonn, J. S. Fernández, J. F.MouraJr., M. E. Madyaningrum, & N. Malherbe (eds), *Handbook of decolonial community psychology* (pp. 1–22). Springer.

Stavrakakis, Y. (2007). *The Lacanian left: Psychoanalysis, theory, politics.* Edinburgh University Press.

Stevens, G. (2007). The international emergence and development of community psychology. In N. Duncan, B. Bowman, A. Naidoo, J. Pillay, & V. Roos (eds), *Community psychology: Analysis, context and action* (pp. 27–50). UCT Press.

Stivala, A., Robins, G., Kashima, Y., & Kirley, M. (2016). Diversity and community can coexist. *American Journal of Community Psychology,* 57(1–2), 243–254.

Tebes, J. K. (2016). Reflections on the future of community psychology from the generations after Swampscott: A commentary and introduction to the special issue. *American Journal of Community Psychology,* 58(3–4), 229–238.

Tomšič, S. (2015a). *Capitalist unconscious: Marx and Lacan.* Verso.

Tomšič, S. (2015b). Psychoanalysis, capitalism, and critique of political economy: Toward a Marxist Lacan. In S. Tomši & A. Zevnik (eds), *Jacques Lacan: Between psychoanalysis and politics* (pp. 146–163). Routledge.

Williams, R. (1975). *The country and the city.* Oxford University Press.

Wood, E. M. (2007). *Democracy against capitalism; Renewing historical materialism.* Aakar Books.

Žižek, S. (1994). *The metastases of enjoyment.* Verso.

Žižek, S. (2022). *Surplus-enjoyment: A guide for the non-perplexed.* Bloomsbury Publishing.

Chapter 4

Unconsciousness-Raising

Introduction

Although there is no unitary way by which to define consciousness-raising (Sarachild, 1978), we can understand it, broadly, as the process of using people's experiences of oppression to inform their political activity within social movements (Sowards & Renegar, 2004). Experience, in other words, is harnessed by consciousness-raising groups as political knowledge (Rosenthal, 1984). Although consciousness-raising does not need to take on a specific formation (the formation of a particular consciousness-raising group tends to be moulded in accordance with the particular struggle in which it is embedded), consciousness-raising has played an integral role in liberation struggles the world over, including radical feminism (Moraga & Anzaldúa, 1983), socialism (Blum, 2008), anti-apartheid activism (Biko, 1978; Moodley, 2018), Latin American anti-imperialism (Fals Borda, 2001; Freire, 1972; Martín-Baró, 1994), decolonial praxis (Lavalette et al., 2018), and many others (see Olcott, 2017; Yu, 2018). Today, consciousness-raising remains central to many of the collectively organised efforts against racial and patriarchal capitalism (e.g. McCarthy & Moon, 2018). In many instances, consciousness-raising is fundamental to the survival of those who participate in it (Woods, 2023).

It is because consciousness-raising signifies the entwinement of the personal and the political that we can understand it as a psycho-political process, that is, a means through which the psychological and the political become enunciated and advanced through the registers of one another (see Hook, 2004). Its psycho-political character has rendered consciousness-raising appealing to those working within the liberation psychology paradigm. Yet, the psycho-political nature of consciousness-raising has also made it a target of psychologisation, that is, a recuperative effort by mainstream psychology to depoliticise and pathologise consciousness-raising's politically progressive mandate (see Parker, 2011). Indeed, much psychology has deployed consciousness-raising as a kind of therapeutic reflection, wherein the subject is encouraged to adjust to capitalism (Kravetz, 1976; Rosenthal, 1984), rather

DOI: 10.4324/9781003612728-4

than recognise the incompatibility of class society and emancipated subjectivity (McGowan, 2013). Psychology, it would seem, has been both an ally and an enemy to those invested in consciousness-raising as a radical political project.

In this chapter, I am concerned with taking consciousness-raising back from mainstream psychology and returning it to the tradition of liberation psychology (or rather, psychoanalytic liberation psychology). Specifically, in what I am calling unconsciousness-raising, we can recognise how unconscious identification and fantasy influence anti-capitalist political organising. Unconsciousness-raising can, in turn, alter the activist subject's relationship to unconscious identifications in accordance with a collectively conceived political agenda. To be clear, unconsciousness-raising is not distinct from consciousness-raising. It represents an approach to consciousness-raising – one that has, in some sense, always existed (see Mitchell, 1971) – wherein repressed knowledges (i.e. traumatic and unconscious knowledges), are understood as having an influence on silenced knowledges (i.e. conscious knowledges that are hidden or obscured by capitalism's oppressive social mechanisms).

In what follows, I briefly touch on the history of consciousness-raising, emphasising how mainstream psychology and liberation psychology have intervened in this history. From here, I attempt to flesh out what it is that I mean by unconsciousness-raising, and how this term has been taken up and appropriated in the past. Then, in exploring some of the political valances of unconsciousness-raising, I consider what this process can tell us about the collective constitution of subjectivity, and how it can trouble static conceptions of reflexivity theory. Following this, and in an attempt to flesh out some of this chapter's theoretical abstractions, I reflect on unconsciousness-raising in the community-engaged work with which I am involved. I conclude by reflecting on what future work in unconsciousness-raising might entail.

Consciousness-Raising and Psychology

The term "consciousness-raising" became popular during the 1960s when the radical wing of the women's liberation movement in the United States began using it as a strategy for political organising (Sowards & Renegar, 2004). For these feminists, most of whom were affiliated with the so-called New Left, consciousness-raising was an attempt to produce a collective understanding of the complexities surrounding women's experiences of patriarchal capitalism. Although it did not encompass a single method, consciousness-raising generally entailed feminist women sharing stories of oppression and exploitation as a way to infuse their political organising with an experiential analysis of the systemic violence being organised against. In other words, experience-as-analysis was drawn on to inform the action that the feminist collective would take to address the gendered nature of structural oppression

(Rosenthal, 1984). As the Redstockings Collective (1970) repeatedly empha-sised, consciousness-raising was intended to demonstrate how individual struggles were connected to a social structure that needed to be resisted and remade collectively. The kinds of knowledges that were availed by con-sciousness-raising, it was argued, could assist feminist women to build self-assurance and strengthen the intersubjective bonds within the feminist movement (Campbell, 2002; Redstockings Collective, 1970; Rosenthal, 1984). As such, consciousness-raising signified an ongoing process for developing feminist strategy, rather than a transient stage within feminist organising (Sarachild, 1978).

Consciousness-raising groups are premised on the dictum that those who experience oppression are experts on such oppression (an insight which was later taken up by feminist standpoint theory; see e.g. Harding, 1986). Con-sequently, consciousness-raising groups were initially intended for those who comprised the oppressed group in question. Sarachild (1978) stresses that consciousness-raising was propelled by a personal-political dialectic that advanced a nuanced feminist agenda through the experiences of individual feminists. One woman's experience would feed into another's, with the most oppressed always being prioritised (Rosenthal, 1984). It was thus with con-sciousness-raising, Sarachild (1978) argued, that feminism could avoid col-lapsing into a reformist campaign or a single-issue movement (see also Sowards & Renegar, 2004). In this regard, consciousness-raising did not seek to rally against a static conception of "false consciousness". Instead, con-sciousness-raising initiatives sought to set the conditions for building a revolutionary consciousness among comrades, creating new subjectivities in the process of building social movements.

Consciousness-raising today has seen several breaks from and continuities with its conceptualisation by New Left feminists. As many have since noted, the feminism of the New Left was, by and large, a white, middle-class, cis-gendered phenomenon, with its consciousness-raising initiatives often reflecting this (see Moraga & Anzaldúa, 1983). While most contemporary consciousness-raising remains the product of anti-capitalist activism (although this is not always the case; see Brooks, 2020), it has moved away from the bourgeois constitution that characterised much of the New Left, drawing, for instance, on decolonising traditions of consciousness-raising (e.g. Biko, 1978; Fals Borda, 2001; Freire, 1972; Martín-Baró, 1994; Moodley, 2018; Suffla & Seedat, 2021). Even within feminist politics, today's con-sciousness-raising initiatives tend to look to the radical Black feminist tradi-tion (e.g. Combahee River Collective, 1995; Moodley, 2018; Moraga & Anzaldúa, 1983) rather than 1960s New Left feminism. Consciousness-raising of this kind is more intersectional, and its consideration of capitalism is alive not only to the patriarchal currents on which capital has always depended, but also the racist, ecocidal, and imperial dimensions of capitalism (see Chapter 1). Today's consciousness-raising activists have not only broadened their political horizons, they have also shifted location. Consciousness-raising is no longer to be found solely within the organisational machinery of social movements. We now see consciousness-raising initiatives everywhere in the public sphere, such as the media, popular culture, communities, and classrooms (see Brown et al., 2017; Sowards & Renegar, 2004).

The discipline of psychology has not been absent in the history of consciousness-raising. However, psychology appears to have engaged consciousness-raising in two politically distinct ways. First, beginning in 1970s group psychology (Rosenthal, 1984), but later spreading to other psychological fields (see Cadaret et al., 2017), psychologists sought to use consciousness-raising as a therapeutic mode of self-reflection (see e.g. Brodsky, 1973; Ellis, 1982; Kravetz et al., 1983; Nassi & Abramowitz, 1978; Weitz, 1982); an end-in-itself rather than an ongoing process of collective politicisation. For these psychologists, consciousness-raising offered a new means by which to empower the individual, often a woman, within the capitalist system. As such, psychologists could use consciousness-raising to produce the competitive, compliant subjectivities that are required by capitalism (see Parker, 2011). Psychology, in short, individualised consciousness-raising and drained it of its political content (Kravetz, 1976; Sarachild, 1978). This can be observed in the ways that psychologists have used consciousness-raising for corporate sensitivity training (Rosenthal, 1984) and executive development (Mirvis, 2008).

There have, however, also been variants of psychology that have engaged with consciousness-raising in the anti-capitalist fashion by which it was intended. Such engagement has been primarily in the fields of community psychology and feminist psychology (see Cheung, 1991; Lykes & Moane, 2009; Montero, 1994; Ruck, 2015; Singh, 2016; Suffla et al., 2015), with some anti-capitalist psychoanalysts also making use of consciousness-raising in this way (Bernardez, 1996). In these instances, Freire's (1972) conception of conscientização has been especially influential. Conscientização denotes an approach to consciousness-raising whereby different groups work together to understand a society's contradictions so that they can take action against oppressive social conditions in an informed manner. Freire saw conscientização as contributing to the fight against capitalist alienation and imperial ideology by rehumanising oppressed subjects and opening up "the possibility of a new praxis, which at the same time makes possible new forms of consciousness" (Martín-Baró, 1994, p. 40). Other psychologists working within the liberation psychology paradigm – especially in community settings (see Suffla & Seedat, 2021) – have drawn on Black Consciousness philosophy's approach to consciousness-raising (Cooper & Ratele, 2018). Black Consciousness rejects the structural denigration of blackness and Black people by emphasising the pride and self-assertion of Black subjectivity. Biko (1978, p. 48), perhaps the most well-known proponent of Black Consciousness philosophy, insisted that "by describing yourself as black you have started on a road towards emancipation, you have committed yourself to fight against all forces that seek to use your blackness as a stamp that marks you out as a subservient being." As such, the Black Consciousness approach to consciousness-raising sought to "produce ... real black people who do not regard themselves as appendages to white society" (Biko, 1978, p. 51).

It would seem, then, that the discipline of psychology has made itself of use to both emancipatory and conservative iterations of consciousness-raising. However, it is important to note that the formulation of consciousness-raising as an anti-capitalist process has had very little to do with psychology (although some psychologists have worked with anti-capitalist consciousness-raising groups), whereas psychology played a pivotal role in formalising consciousness-raising as a corporatised method of capitalist adaptation (Rosenthal, 1984).

What, then, of Unconsciousness-Raising and Liberation Psychology?

Consciousness-raising aims to recover and develop a politicised and collective understanding of oppression (Campbell, 2002). And yet, as we know, sometimes conscious knowledge is not enough. As those in the climate justice movement have repeatedly asked: "Why are we so passive when we know so much?" (Malm, 2023, p. 18). Thus, in addition to uncovering conscious knowledges and experiences that have been hidden or silenced by oppressive social apparatuses, consciousness-raising might also attend to repressed, unconscious knowledges that are 'known' on bodily and psychic levels. A consciousness-raising of this kind takes matters of the unconscious especially seriously.

Unconsciousness-raising initiatives strive to recognise how unconscious desire obstructs and/or advances the political goals of the collective, thereby allowing subjects to change their relationship to their desires, or indeed use these desires to foster solidarity and bolster their commitment to a collectively constituted anti-capitalist project – one whose form is determined by the particularities of existing struggle. Unconsciousness-raising can be practised among specific groups or across different groups. It may encompass free association, dream interpretation, or any other mode of psychoanalytic inquiry.

Unconsciousness-raising is an inherently collective endeavour precisely because the unconscious is not an isolated affair. The unconscious, as we know, emerges when the subject enters into language, or what Lacanians call the symbolic order (Parker, 2011). In other words, the unconscious is present in the other side of the language that we speak, and because language fails to encapsulate the full meaning of that which it seeks to signify, the unconscious points to how psychological subjects are connected via a common experience of subjective splitting, whereby their ideas, words, and actions never form exactly as they intend (Parker & Pavón-Cuéllar, 2021). Lacan (2001) himself described the unconscious as unknowable knowledge. We can encircle the unknowability of this knowledge by making connections between the gaps and inconsistencies within spoken language, thus revealing the mechanisms of the unconscious rather than "unconscious content" as such (Stavrakakis, 2007). The unconscious, in short, indicates how the outside (e.g. past relationships, society, history) is always also inside the split subject, forming the "unspoken ground of our collective being" (Parker & Pavón-Cuéllar, 2021, p. 132). Ali (2020, p. 42) insists that "This understanding of the unconscious implies that psychoanalysis is never really concerned with individual problems ... but in showing how what appear to be the most intimate and internal problems are in fact already inscribed from the very beginning in a socio-symbolic field." Accordingly, the unconscious is an ethical, place-bound concept rather than a purely epistemological one (Tupinambá, 2021).

To speak of the social constitution of the unconscious is not to declare that all subjects experience unconscious repression in the same way. For the unconsciousness-raising group, there is a tension between the formation of the individual's unconscious desires and traumas, and the unconscious mechanisms operating within the group. This tension is not to be done away with by focusing on the unconscious at either the group or the individual level. Rather, unconsciousness-raising initiatives can attempt to navigate and traverse this tension by engaging carefully with what Fanon (1986 [1967]) called sociogeny, that is, the understanding that psychic phenomena are produced and reproduced through sociohistorical processes. The psychic effects of racism are, for instance, the result of an anti-Black capitalist society. Addressing sociogenic trauma – which speaks to the internalisation of violent social structures – thus requires socio-political rather than individualistic interventions. In taking seriously sociogenic trauma, unconsciousness-raising groups look to foster solidarity between differently and unevenly traumatised subjects who are committed to a shared anti-capitalist political project. Although I do not necessarily experience sociogenic trauma in the same way as my comrades, there is nonetheless a commonly experienced repression under capitalism that structures our individual traumas, and we can connect with one another by committing to taking action against this repression, while at the same time recognising the injustice inherent to different, yet interconnected, sociogenic traumas.

Unconsciousness-raising is not a moralistic exercise that aims to induce judgment among comrades. Rather, unconsciousness-raising is an ethical process whose goal (i.e. strengthening an individual's political commitment and fostering solidarity) is achieved through the recognition of the structuring effects of the unconscious, that is, how unconscious desire shapes, deepens, and undermines conscious activity. Those involved in unconsciousness-raising open themselves up to being affected by the vulnerability of their comrades (see Lear, 2005), and advance collective struggles by recognising the humanity and psychic failures of themselves and those with whom they struggle – particularly in the context of struggle (Malherbe, 2021). The unconsciousness-raising group is, therefore, determined by struggle, and is not especially concerned with retaining a particular form or distinctive identification precisely because social change is always also connected with individual changes within the group (see Parker & Pavón-Cuéllar, 2021). Our ability to act together, politically, is entwined with how we relate to each other as individual subjects.

If unconsciousness-raising is not a moralistic undertaking, it is also not an idealistic one. We should not underestimate the psychic potency and (re) traumatising potential of unconscious identifications, formations, and dynamics. Indeed, unconsciousness-raising carries the risk of fracturing and psychically injuring members of the collective. Unconsciousness-raising groups should, therefore, anticipate defences between comrades (or, perhaps rather, potential comrades) that can manifest, for example, in feelings of resentment and envy. For unconsciousness-raising collectives, internal tensions can be used to hold radical, grassroots politics accountable to a common, collectively determined set of commitments. Enunciating the tensions that exist within a group is not, then, to move towards tolerating any and all tension. Rather, drawing attention to group tension can highlight to group members the limits of solidarity – what should not be tolerated within a group committed to emancipation. Although this carries the risk of (re) traumatising comrades and splintering social movements, many of which are already precarious, consolidating socio-political change-making in ways that reflect the liberatory commitments of a group necessitates taking this risk. Unconsciousness-raising is useful precisely because it seeks to bring conflict into the open, using it to propel movements and their political commitments. As such, we guard against repressing conflict and allowing it to erode political movements from within.

Unconsciousness-raising should not be understood as entirely separate from – or as signifying an alternative to – consciousness-raising as it is usually conceived. As Woods (2023) emphasises, unconsciousness-raising has always existed as a particular approach to consciousness-raising. Mitchell (1971, p. 61) writes that consciousness-raising praxis allows people to speak what is so often unspoken, facilitating "the release of anger, anxiety, the struggle of proclaiming the painful and transforming it into the political" (Mitchell, 1971, p. 61). This, she argues, aligns consciousness-raising with the psychoanalytic preoccupation with the unconscious. Leland (1988, p. 98) similarly insists that consciousness-raising allows groups to "discover facets of internalised oppression by 'showing up' the sexual ideology that affects our desires, feelings, thoughts, and valuations". The conscious hidden knowledges with which the consciousness-raising group is preoccupied are, after all, structured by the repressed unconscious mechanisms within the group (Bion, 1961). Moreover, as Stevens (2023) insists, our conscious political commitments guide how we engage with unconscious processes, and to what purpose this engagement is put. We therefore cannot neatly separate the unconscious from what is conscious. Contrary to those in the psychoanalytic tradition who critique consciousness-raising's approach to human emancipation as one that demands our full knowledge of a situation (e.g. McGowan, 2013), the history of consciousness-raising shows that it is a process that welcomes adaptation, movement, and new insights. Matters of the unconscious can be, and certainly have been, harnessed to inform consciousness-raising's mandate of committing activist subjects to emancipatory politics – a point that Woods (2023) and Stevens (2023) have pushed me to make more strongly here than I had done in a previous version of this chapter.

Regardless of the fact that unconsciousness-raising has always in some respect been part of consciousness-raising's political mandate, the term *unconsciousness-raising* is rarely used explicitly. Although the term can be found in several psychoanalytic texts, it remains, for the most part, poorly conceptualised, apolitical, and/or deployed in accordance with neoliberal ideology. For some psychoanalysts, unconsciousness-raising has been used to describe psychoanalysis as a therapeutic technique (e.g. Jacobs, 2001). Others have attributed unconsciousness-raising to certain psychoanalytic approaches, such as "Zenalys" (Southgate, 1983) or feminist psychoanalysis more broadly (see Blackman et al., 2008). Unconsciousness-raising has also been drawn on for particular purposes within psychoanalytic inquiry, such as research into the implicit association test (Casad et al., 2013), efforts to advance the wellbeing of those working in public sphere organisations (Winship, 2005), and interventions into the gender divisions that exist in the corporate sphere (Reskin, 2005). By and large, though, unconsciousness-raising has not been used to describe collective efforts to organise against racial and patriarchal capitalism (see Ryan & Trevithick, 1988 for a notable exception here, however even in this instance unconsciousness-raising remains somewhat under-developed).

Unconsciousness-raising is not the only way to interrogate unconscious processes within group contexts. The A. K. Rice Institute and the Tavistock Institute, for instance, have produced work in this area (Rustin & Armstrong, 2019). Unconsciousness-raising can certainly benefit, conceptually, from the insights garnered by organisations like these. Bion's (1961) work on basic assumptions, for example, may be useful for understanding the individual-collective dialectic, the will to action, and the flows of power within a particular group. However, its uncompromising anti-capitalist commitments set unconsciousness-rising groups apart from many (but certainly not all) of those affiliated with A. K. Rice and Tavistock. Unconsciousness-raising is, first and foremost, an anti-capitalist resource for grassroots social movements, which jars with some of the work in corporate management that takes place in the Rice and Tavistock Institutes (again, though, this does not represent all of the work in these Institutes, some of which is guided by feminist praxis). If unconsciousness-raising were to be co-opted and used for anything other than strengthening anti-capitalist resistance efforts, it would cede its definitional anchor, and become something else. Unconsciousness-raising is distinguished by its anti-capitalist political commitments.

Fanon (1986 [1967], p. 100) reflects that "As a psychoanalyst, I should help my patient to become conscious of his [sic] unconscious and abandon his [sic] attempts at a hallucinatory whitening, but also to act in the direction of a change in the social structure." Psychological practitioners certainly bring particular skills to the unconsciousness-raising group. However, they need not remain at a clinical distance from this group. On the contrary, because the psy-disciplines are so entwined with capitalism, it is likely that these practitioners – no matter how anti-capitalist their conscious identifications may be – have unconscious investments in the capitalist order. Accordingly, when consciousness-raising centres the unconscious to form unconscious-ness-raising, such desires are held accountable to the political goals to which the unconsciousness-raising collective commits (Malherbe, 2021).

It is worth emphasising Lear's (2005) point that because we cannot *know* the contents of the unconscious (i.e. the unconscious always resists symbolisation; Lacan, 2001), the goal of psychoanalysis is to *experience* the unconscious in the here-and-now. When political subjects take responsibility for their desires and recognise how the unconscious structures their conscious political activism, they are afforded practical insights and skills that can enhance how they work, struggle, and forge solidarity with one another as comrades. Unconsciousness-raising is, accordingly, an attempt to practise psychoanalytic liberation psychology at the level of the political community (see González & Peltz, 2021), advancing emancipatory politics via a psychological, and often very challenging, reckoning with this community – sometimes reconceptualising the community in the process.

Unconsciousness-Raising and Subjectivity

Unconsciousness-raising is always willed towards moving the subjects who comprise a political collective to disidentify with the identifications offered by the capitalist symbolic order. This does not mean exiting from the symbolic order as such, nor is it to foster a perpetual disidentification that can only but stifle actioning one's anti-capitalist commitments. It is instead to embrace the fractured-becoming of subjectivity that the unconscious reveals, seeking to show which identifications can impede the political project with which the collective identifies (e.g. the capitalist subjectivity of the compliant, unpaid reproductive worker must be rejected by those who identify with intersectional socialism). In other words, unconsciousness-raising initiatives accept that we do not fully cohere with the subjectivities offered to us by capitalism, and advances struggles through this misfitting, striving to alter the symbolic order from within (Malherbe, 2021). In this, we move away from illusions of mastery by accepting what Lacanians refer to as our symbolic castration, while also acknowledging the materiality out of which identity emerges – refusing to *become* an identity. I cannot ignore the material advantages that are bestowed upon me as a white, male subject, but I can refuse the ways by which capitalism hails this subjectivity. We saw this, for example, when protesting students in South Africa responded to the threat of police violence by situating white students on the parameters of their collective, thus forming a symbolic "human shield" (Sherriff, 2015). A tactic of this sort (which spoke directly to the South African Police Service's well-documented use of violence against Black protesters) is indicative of how the material privileges bestowed onto symbolic identity can be re-deployed to advance political commitments. To take an example mentioned earlier, the Black Consciousness Movement in South Africa refused the symbolic degradations that the apartheid state imposed onto blackness, and instead infused blackness with pride and the insurgent power necessary to dismantle apartheid (see Biko, 1978; Moodley, 2018). By working with people to embrace symbolic castration in these ways, unconsciousness-raising has the potential to change the subject's relationship with colonial capitalist identification as well as the superstructural norms out of which this identification emerges. Although unconsciousness-raising may prove therapeutic for some (and will certainly entail psychological anguish for many), it is – in this very particular sense – a political rather than a clinical process.

Unconsciousness-raising does not do away with fantasy or engage fantasy as merely false consciousness. Although, as we saw in Chapter 2, fantasy can conceal the subject's contradictions through enjoyable false images of wholeness and mastery (Freud, 1924), it can also take subjects beyond the limitations of a symbolic structure, challenging this structure and even offering alternatives to it. Therefore, far from being predetermined, the political valance of fantasy depends on how we organise our enjoyment (McGowan, 2013), a Lacanian term that, we may recall from Chapters 2 and 3, refers to an unconscious energy that invests a pleasurable quality into the displeasure that accompanies not quite fitting in with a prevailing symbolic order (Stavrakakis, 2007). Fantasy can envision emancipation and enjoyment beyond the available means of symbolisation, wresting unconscious attachment away from an unjust symbolic and social order. By taking seriously the transgressive potential of fantasy, unconsciousness-raising can broaden the political horizons towards which activists aspire and through which their political subjectivities are formed, guarding against compulsively driven repetitions within processes of emancipatory future-building (see Lear, 2005).

It is because subjectivity always, at some level, fails to cohere with a symbolically determined ego-ideal, that unconsciousness-raising can allow subjects to engage with one another as comrades through this mutual symbolic failure (see Ruti, 2008; Stavrakakis, 2007). We can access the Other as a comrade precisely because the Other is never entirely foreclosed symbolically (Dean, 2019; Malherbe, 2021). As psychoanalysis is concerned with analysing subjectivity rather than 'treating it' (González & Peltz, 2021), unconscious-ness-raising rejects mainstream psychology's pathologising of subjective con-tradiction and instead uses these contradictions to strengthen solidarity (i.e. how subjects commit to one another as well as the emancipatory anti-capi-talist project that binds them together as comrades). In this way, we can begin to approach *unité de rupture*: "the moment when the contradictions so reinforce one another as to coalesce into the conditions for a revolutionary change" (Mitchell, 1971, p. 101). Yet, as noted earlier, engaging contradiction in this manner is not conflict-free. Trauma plays a central role in how people embrace symbolic inconsistences within the self and the Other. The point to be made, however, is that if contradictions are engaged sensitively and in a manner that aligns with the group's broader political commitments, they can strengthen the solidarity bond between group members.

Unconsciousness-raising can compel subjects to identify with anti-capitalist politics not via the promise of psychic fulfilment, but through the enjoyment derived from the transgressions inherent to such a politics. A politics of this sort admits the limitations of an emancipatory project premised on subvert-ing capitalism in its totality, and instead strives to identify contradictions within this system so that activists can work to exacerbate these contra-dictions, and thus transform social systems from within by forcing them to reckon with their own logic (McGowan, 2013; Stavrakakis, 2007). For instance, capitalist ideology claims to honour the freedom of the individual, yet global austerity, surveillance, and imperial militarism have seen to the denial of the most basic dignities that individuals require to exercise freedom (e.g. healthcare, education, nutrition, housing, life, connection, freedom). Just as the activist subject can use unconsciousness-raising to advance anti-capitalist politics by embracing a refusal to cohere with capitalism's symbolic order, these same subjects can use the contradictions within oppressive systems to challenge these systems and turn them against themselves.

Through unconsciousness-raising, subjects can work together to radicalise subjectivity by embracing their psychic fragmentation, using anti-capitalist politics not as a means of settling this fragmentation, but as a transgressive and enjoyable means by which to address sociogenic trauma and the con-tradictions inherent to capitalism. Similarly, fantasy cannot be eradicated from subjectivity, but we can change how we relate to and enjoy fantasy by using it to push anti-capitalist visions of liberation beyond the dominant symbolic order (Stavrakakis, 2007). The ethical dimension of unconscious-ness-raising thus lies in how it assists subjects to live and act in the company of others who are committed to a common anti-capitalist project (Dean, 2019). Nonetheless, the manner by which unconsciousness-raising engages subjectivity remains psychologically challenging, and potentially traumatic.

Unconsciousness-raising also cannot, in itself, create revolutionary subjects. Instead, it can facilitate the kinds of difficult reflection required to develop a revolution in subjectivity (Parker, 2011). It is, therefore, through unconsciousness-raising that political subjects can take responsibility for their desires, that is, remain accountable to how subjectivity is embodied and organised in the context of emancipatory political activity.

Unconsciousness-Raising with and Against Reflexivity Theory

Reflexivity theory has been very influential for many working within liberation psychology (Lykes & Moane, 2009). Broadly, reflexivity can be defined as a process of developing a politicised self-awareness that influences how one acts (Pringle & Thorpe, 2017). A heightened awareness of and engagement with my social privileges, reflexivity theory posits, can ensure that I act to flatten unequal relations of power. Male-bodied persons engaged in reflexivity can, for instance, work to combat cis-heteronormative social structures by continually engaging with the kinds of undue power that patriarchy has bestowed upon them, which often means giving up certain privileges. It is not difficult to see how reflexivity theory aligns with the project of consciousness-raising. Critical consciousness tends to arise out of a reflexive encounter with one's social positionality (Suffla et al., 2015). As Pillow (2003, p. 178) recounts in her well-known description of reflexivity in research settings: "the researcher [is] to be critically conscious through [a] personal accounting of how the researcher's self-location (across – for example – gender, race, class, sexuality, ethnicity, nationality), position, and interests influence all stages of the research process."

While psychoanalytic work has not neglected reflexivity theory (see Aron, 2000; Brown, 2006), such work is rarely political and community-oriented (i. e. constituted as psychoanalytic liberation psychology). Unconsciousness-raising, I argue, pushes reflexivity theory into the politically progressive terrain on which it was initially conceived by exploring the deconstructive potentialities of reflexivity, whereby the limits of human consciousness and knowledge production within the context of collective struggle are foregrounded. Unconsciousness-raising, therefore, rejects the use of reflexivity as mere self-knowledge that can be used to bolster the subject's self-image and/or reaffirm how the subject wishes to be gazed upon (see Hook, 2013). Realising politics through such narcissism can sublimate political action into an enjoyable – seemingly endless – cycle of guilty thoughts (Lear, 2005), which is to say, it can instate a self-destructive politics propelled by fear rather than anti-capitalist visions of emancipation. Instead, unconsciousness-raising draws on reflexivity theory to better understand how "the other reveals me to myself" (Fanon, 2018, p. 219).

Looking to Lacanian psychoanalytic theory, we might say that unconsciousness-raising rejects modes of reflexivity that privilege empty speech, that is, ego-affirming self-narratives that either endorse the subject's imaginary self-image (Hook, 2013), or perceive the Other's imagined wholeness as a threat to one's own (McGowan, 2013). Although empty speech can be reflexive, such reflexivity and any critical directions it may take are controlled by the speaker. Unconsciousness-raising thus offers a way to move reflexivity theory's focus away from empty speech and towards full speech, wherein knowledge is not located in the subject's conscious locution, but within the unintended interpretations, mistakes, and slips that occur within the subject's speech. It is with full speech that the subject's words are returned to them in order to disrupt their self-image through an awareness of their unconscious desire (see Hook, 2013), attempting to incorporate into conscious knowledge the limits of knowing (Stavrakakis, 2007). Through full speech, I may come to realise that my identity as an anti-capitalist psychologist is contradicted by an unconscious desire to attain the kinds of material and cultural privileges that successful psychologists accrue under capitalism (Malherbe, 2021). The point here is not to evoke guilt within the subject, nor is it to posit that the use of full speech is without trauma or tension. Instead, coming into full speech is a psychically challenging process by which the subject can take responsibility for their desires, rather than merely acknowledge them.

Unconsciousness-raising does not harness reflexivity in an attempt to *know thyself* through repeated, potentially enjoyable, self-flagellation. Rather, by engaging with reflexivity through full speech, activists can challenge oppressive symbolic logic (and its operation on the unconscious) by confronting how they relate to their enjoyment and giving up attempts at attaining complete mastery over the self (Stavrakakis, 2007), challenging as this may be. In this, unconsciousness-raising initiatives honour Pillow's (2003) often-forgotten call to use the reflexive process to render the unfamiliar exactly what it is: unfamiliar. We may then better recognise and take responsibility for the structuring effects that the unconscious has on our conscious attempts to action an anti-capitalist political programme.

Case Reflection

In what follows, I discuss the general structure of a particular unconsciousness-raising group and the political implications thereof. My reflections do not represent an ideal model for unconsciousness-raising, nor do they serve as a guidebook for conducting unconsciousness-raising groups. Like all unconsciousness-raising initiatives, the one I recount here contains within it a host of challenges, problems, and contradictions.

Following on from a participatory action research (PAR) project where residents from a marginalised community in South Africa engaged with the effects of structural violence in their community, several colleagues (all of whom were outsiders to this community and represented a broad range of identities and class backgrounds) and I worked with social movement actors from the community to organise a series of meetings. At these meetings, movement activists and other community members worked with one another to organise grassroots initiatives that could address the kinds of structural violence identified within the PAR project. Specifically, the meetings focused on how the South African state could be pushed to support cooperative business models in the community, improve amenities in the community, provide social housing, and upgrade the community's sanitation system. As my colleagues and I have experience in group facilitation in and beyond this community, no internal processes took place between us prior to these meetings. As Woods (2023) notes, this lack of preparation was a rather problematic oversight and may have resulted in insufficient containment.

Although everyone living in the community was invited to these meetings, they were initially attended almost exclusively by men. These male attendees – many of whom were expressly and consciously committed to gender equity – proclaimed that they were distressed at such androcentrism. They were, however, unsure how to address this issue in a meaningful way. Eventually, a feminist meeting attendee suggested that when inviting community members to these meetings, people should be encouraged to bring their children with them. As childrearing in South Africa – like in many other places – remains a form of reproductive labour that is arbitrarily and unfairly expected of women, the invitation to bring children to the meetings meant that, soon enough, women attendees outnumbered men.

Despite many of the male attendees' consciously professed feminism, the inclusion of women in these meetings appeared to cause considerable tension. Several of these men interrupted the female attendees, dismissing their ideas and concerns while assuming leadership and control over group decision-making. These men, we might say, appeared to be defending against their unconscious anxiety over symbolic castration. In turn, many of the women in attendance began to express feelings of frustration precisely because they were being denied the ability to enter meaningfully into the group's professed anti-capitalist symbolic order, that is, to take up the language required to embody political subjectivity in this space. At this juncture, my colleagues and I suggested that these group tensions be addressed through an open and unconstrained discussion; what I have since come to understand as unconsciousness-raising.

This particular unconsciousness-raising session occurred over the course of a single two-hour meeting. However, as we will see, its effects lasted beyond this. To begin the session, my colleague put it to the group that we had noticed that there was friction between group members. As such, everyone in the group was invited to speak their mind as freely as possible. We requested that people not interrupt one another (as this would impede full speech), and that the discussion need not proceed in a linear, or turn-taking, fashion. Rather, people could respond to each other in a back-and-forth manner. Although the group members initiated the session with polite, empty speech, it was when they entered into full speech that the unconscious nature of the group tensions was made clear. While it is unethical to recount full excerpts from this discussion, it is – for our purposes – suffice to note that several male group members used the word "brothers" in place of "comrades" (despite the latter being the convention within the social movement). Several other men in the group alluded to women in the community being by and large less interested in politics than men, using sexist tropes to do so. Some male group members also expressed that the kinds of childrearing activities that now took place at the meetings (e.g. breastfeeding and diaperchanging) were distracting and apolitical. In short, for many of the male group attendees, the presence of the feminised subject was anxiety-provoking precisely because this subject represented a symbol of castration; a seeming threat to the perceived mastery, power, and identity associated with masculinised subjectivity. This is what Gana (2023, p. 41) calls melancholy manhood, "a loss or crisis of old conceptions of manhood [which] has taken place but has not been accompanied with the parallel and adequate psychosocial and hermeneutic readjustment necessary for its resolution".

Desire, Lacan (2001) insists, is sustained by the subject's foundational psychic lack, unlike anxiety, which arises from an absence of lack. It is because anxiety is too overwhelming, experienced as too much, that we try to cover it with images of completeness that ultimately fail. Where an anxiety-driven politics guards against the symbolic threats that cause anxiety, a politics of desire seeks to perpetually make and remake itself (McGowan, 2013), and thus has the potential to accommodate a range of different struggles (Malherbe, 2021). As a facilitator of an unconsciousness-raising group, my role was not to impose a moralistically determined assessment of the group discussion. Instead, I encouraged group members to bring into the discussion the expansive politics of desire to which their group was committed (i.e. an intersectional socialist agenda that insisted on justice for all who live in and beyond this community). As such, many of the women in attendance acknowledged that they were committed to the same material struggles as the male activists, however, the male activists appeared reluctant to incorporate feminist struggles around gender-based violence and unpaid reproductive labour into the movement's symbolic order. Feminist struggle, these women insisted, needed to be explicitly and consciously brought into the movement. In this way, anxious patriarchal fantasies of liberation were undermined by a politics of desire, wherein anti-capitalist liberation was collectively reconstituted through different desires within the group.

As expected, these discussions often exacerbated group tensions. Several group members became irate with one another, while others spoke candidly about personal experiences of trauma which, they emphasised, were fundamentally political matters that needed to be taken seriously by activist movements in the community. In response, a small number of group members dismissed these accounts of trauma, deeming them beyond the scope of social movement politics. In turn, after the meeting, some attendees requested individual counselling. It may, indeed, be useful to initiate smaller group discussions with those who experience marginalisation in the context of the larger group (keeping in mind also that those in the group who dismissed the trauma of others may be repeating traumas of their own). In these small groups, people can work with one another to articulate the conditions upon which they will enter into the solidarity relation with the larger group. These conditions must be uncompromising and should reflect the larger group's desire-driven politics of emancipation. In this way, the larger group's collectively constituted political commitments can be used to hold individual group members accountable.

Although the outcomes of this unconsciousness-raising process were not immediate or especially clear, several lingering effects were noted in follow-up meetings with the group. For example, at a meeting that followed this unconsciousness-raising session, several community members – some male, but mostly female – repeatedly challenged the apparent universality of the male activist subject that was being asserted by some in the group. By demanding that gendered sociogenic issues (e.g. domestic violence and unsupported childcare) be incorporated into the group's political programme, the symbolic consistency of male subjectivity – and its assumed universality – was disturbed. The masculinised activist subjectivity was, in other words, refracted and remade by invoking the struggles faced by other desiring subjects. Hollander (2023) observed something similar in her psychoanalytic liberation psychology work that took place during the US-backed dictatorships in Latin America, wherein activists were able to challenge the masculinisation of their movements by setting up regular reflection sessions.

Another effect of this unconsciousness-raising session was observed in how the solidarity bond within the group was disrupted and remade at subsequent meetings. For example, although the sociogenic trauma that group members discussed was often gendered (e.g. women's experiences of spousal abuse and men's experiences of police brutality), many group members connected these traumas with a commonly experienced material depravity rooted in capitalist structures of accumulation. The racialised nature of South Africa's political economy was also stressed. Meeting attendees – all of whom identified as Black – linked their gendered traumas to broader systems of white supremacy in the country, recounting specific experiences of racism that group members had endured, many of which occurred in the workplace. Although some group members retreated into the mythologised psychic solace promised by an anxious, masculinised activist subjectivity, for others, trauma was acknowledged by embracing a shared vulnerability (see Hollander, 2023). Solidarity-making was not, in these instances, premised on the mythic wholeness promised by the hegemonic identifications made available and required by capitalism. Instead, the solidarity bond was forged through how group members did not cohere with capitalism's dominant identifications and how they were injured, in different ways, by the imposition of these identifications. Emancipatory desires for new identifications were then forged between differently suffering subjects in the group.

I was not exempt from the sorts of reflexivity with which the group engaged. As one community member explained it, middle-class white people like me had played a central role in materially disenfranchising people living in this community since its foundation in the apartheid era. As such, some community members remarked that when meetings like these were facilitated by a white person like me, the meetings felt somewhat uncanny: "that species of the frightening that goes back to what was once well known and had long been familiar" (Freud, 2003, p. 124). Certainly, my presence may well have inhibited full speech within the group. It is also possible that group members altered their responses and/or reacted to me in ways that I did not notice. Additionally, my interactions with individual group members may have been unconsciously influenced by the privileges bestowed upon me as a white, cisgendered man working within and, in some ways, benefitting from a vociferous and structurally violent capitalist social order. I, too, may have unconsciously reproduced the patriarchal tropes that I had consciously identified in others as problematic. Therefore, it is not only possible that in some instances I hindered, rather than assisted, the group in realising its political goals, but also that the group might have functioned more effectively had I not been present. Understanding the effects of my presence and unconscious responses in the group requires longitudinal analytic attention as well as the establishment of processes that hold me, as a facilitator, accountable to the group's anti-capitalist political programme. In partially addressing some of these issues, the group decided that my role in these meetings, and therefore in organising community struggles, should be to assist group members in engaging with the group's internal tensions and – via my institutional affiliation – avail the necessary resources required for political organising, such as a meeting venue and transportation. Although my symbolic identity could not be altogether obliterated, it was possible to draw on some of the material privileges of this identity in ways that allowed me to participate in, rather than disengage from, consolidating the group's political commitments and emancipatory desires.

There were undoubtedly limitations inherent to this unconsciousness-raising process. Many of the group tensions persist and unconscious patriarchal undercurrents continue to structure many political meetings. It is also difficult to engage adequately with the considerable trauma presented by individual group members and to meaningfully address the – often hidden or repressed – marginalisation processes operating in the group. Moreover, although I have focused here on the gendered dimension of some of the group members' full speech, the parapraxes within this speech revealed several other unconscious identifications and attachments. It is difficult to assess the effectiveness of this unconsciousness-raising intervention with respect to the group's political goals and activist activity. Many of these goals and activities (e.g. organising protest events and pickets; planning community campaigns; establishing communication with the state) were realised, and likely would have been realised had this intervention not taken place. Nonetheless, I believe that the unconsciousness-raising process contributed to strengthening the solidarity bond within the group, and thus assisted in broadening the group's political commitments and garnering appeal for its anti-capitalist programme. This was due to the fact that the stiflingly anxious, gendered nature of the group's symbolic order was not able to function as it had prior to the unconsciousness-raising intervention. It is in these effects, internal to the group, that we can observe the political use-value of unconsciousness-raising.

Conclusion

In speaking about the consciousness-raising efforts of the New Left, Freeman (1972) warned against what she called the tyranny of structurelessness, whereby attempts to establish an absence of hierarchy within consciousness-raising groups allowed the group's unacknowledged hierarchies to operate all the more effectively. The tyranny of structurelessness can also be understood in relation to the unconscious. If, indeed, the structuring effects of the unconscious are ignored, the grip that unconscious mechanisms hold over anti-capitalist political processes may be strengthened.

In this chapter, I argue for unconsciousness-raising, an approach to consciousness-raising that seeks to put psychoanalytic liberation psychology to the task of bringing about greater cohesion within political collectives by identifying the kinds of compulsively driven repeats and identifications that mimic the logic of the capitalist symbolic order being challenged. Anxious conceptions of a singular or fixed vision of emancipation are, therefore, rejected for an approach to politics, solidarity, and subjectivity that is defined by the flows of emancipatory desire within the group. Through unconsciousness-raising, political subjects can move towards taking responsibility for their desires in relation to the broader anti-capitalist project to which they are committed. This, I hope to have made clear, is by no means a simple or conflict-free process. It is tremendously difficult and emotionally charged.

I have offered in this chapter some nascent provocations into how psychoanalytic insights can be applied to politically committed and community-engaged psychological work, that is, to the practice of psychoanalytic liberation psychology. Much of what I consider here reflects my own biases and myopias. There are, of course, myriad other ways by which to harness the unconscious to inform progressive political activity. There is considerable work that can be done on a variety of different topics (e.g. organising across different political issues; strengthening an intersectional anti-capitalist politics; building intra-community solidarity), and from a range of perspectives (e.g. Marxian, feminist, decolonial, anarchist, Kleinian, Jungian, and/or Freudian). I have, therefore, considered in this chapter only some of the possibilities and exploratory avenues for unconsciousness-raising within psychoanalytic liberation psychology.

References

Ali, N. B. (2020). *Psychoanalysis and the love of Arabic: Hall of mirrors*. Edinburgh University Press.

Aron, L. (2000). Self-reflexivity and the therapeutic action of psychoanalysis. *Psychoanalytic Psychology*, 17(4), 667–689.

Bernardez, T. (1996). The quiet revolution: Consciousness raising and psychoanalytic practice. *Bulletin of the Menninger Clinic*, 60(4), 480–487.

Biko, S. (1978). *I write what I like: Selected writings*. University of Chicago Press.

Bion, W. R. (1961). *Experiences in groups and other papers*. Tavistock.

Blackman, L., Cromby, J., Hook, D., Papadopoulos, D., & Walkerdine, V. (2008). Creating subjectivities. *Subjectivity*, 22(1), 1–27.

Blum, D. (2008). Socialist consciousness raising and Cuba's School to the Countryside Program. *Anthropology & Education Quarterly*, 39(2), 141–160.

Brodsky, A. M. (1973). The consciousness-raising group as a model for therapy with women. *Psychotherapy: Theory, Research & Practice*, 10(1), 24–29.

Brooks, M. A. (2020). It's okay to be white: Laundering white supremacy through a colorblind victimized white race-consciousness raising campaign. *Sociological Spectrum*, 40(6), 400–416.

Brown, J. (2006). Reflexivity in the research process: Psychoanalytic observations. *International Journal of Social Research Methodology*, 9(3), 181–197.

Brown, M., Ray, R., Summers, E., & Fraistat, N. (2017). #SayHerName: A case study of intersectional social media activism. *Ethnic and Racial Studies*, 40(11), 1831–1846.

Cadaret, M. C., Hartung, P. J., Subich, L. M., & Weigold, I. K. (2017). Stereotype threat as a barrier to women entering engineering careers. *Journal of Vocational Behavior*, 99, 40–51.

Campbell, K. K. (2002). Consciousness-raising: Linking theory, criticism, and practice. *Rhetoric Society Quarterly*, 32(1), 45–64.

Casad, B. J., Flores, A. J., & Didway, J. D. (2013). Using the implicit association test as an unconsciousness raising tool in psychology. *Teaching of Psychology*, 40(2), 118–123.

Cheung, F. M. (1991). Consciousness-raising of gender issues in clinical psychology training: A community psychology approach. *Feminism & Psychology*, 1(1), 93–95.

Combahee River Collective. (1995). Combahee River Collective statement. In B. Guy-Sheftall (ed.), *Words of fire: An anthology of African American feminist thought* (pp. 232–240). New Press.

Cooper, S., & Ratele, K. (2018). The Black Consciousness psychology of Steve Biko. In S. Fernando, & R. Moodley (eds), *Global psychologies: Mental health and the Global South* (pp. 245–260). Palgrave Macmillan.

Dean, J. (2019). *Comrade: An essay on political belonging*. Verso.

Ellis, D. G. (1982). Relational stability and change in women's consciousness-raising groups. *Women's Studies in Communication*, 5(2), 77–87.

Fals Borda, O. (2001). Participatory (action) research in social theory: Origins and challenges. In P. Reason & H. Bradbury (eds), *Handbook of action research* (pp. 27–37). Sage.

Fanon, F. (1986 [1967]). *Black skin, white masks*. Pluto.

Fanon, F. (2018). *Alienation and freedom*. Bloomsbury.

Freeman, J. (1972). The tyranny of structurelessness. In A. Koedt, E. Levine, & A. Rapone (eds), *Radical feminism* (285–299). Quadrangle.

Freire, P. (1972). *Pedagogy of the oppressed*. Herder and Herder.

Freud, S. (1924). 'Wild' psycho-analysis. In J. Strachey (ed., trans.), *The standard edition of the complete psychological works of Sigmund Freud, vol. 11*. Hogarth Press.

Freud, S. (2003). *The uncanny*. Penguin Books.

Gana, N. (2023). *Melancholy acts: Defeat and cultural critique in the Arab world*. Fordham University Press.

González, F. J., & Peltz, R. (2021). Community psychoanalysis: Collaborative practice as intervention. *Psychoanalytic Dialogues*, 31(4), 409–427.

Harding, S. G. (1986). *The science question in feminism*. Cornell University Press.

Hollander, N. C. (2023). *Uprooted minds: A social psychoanalysis for precarious times*. Routledge.

Hook, D. (2004). Frantz Fanon, Steve Biko and 'psychopolitics'. In D. Hook (ed.), *Critical psychology* (pp. 84–114). University of Cape Town Press.

Hook, D. (2013). *(Post)apartheid conditions: Psychoanalysis and social formation*. Palgrave Macmillan.

Jacobs, T. J. (2001). On misreading and misleading patients: Some reflections on communications, miscommunications and countertransference enactments. *International Journal of Psychoanalysis*, 82(4), 653–669.

Kravetz, D. F. (1976). Consciousness-raising groups and group psychotherapy: Alternative mental health resources for women. *Psychotherapy: Theory, Research & Practice*, 13(1), 66–71.

Kravetz, D., Marecek, J., & Finn, S. E. (1983). Factors influencing women's participation in consciousness-raising groups. *Psychology of Women Quarterly*, 7(3), 257–271.

Lacan, J. (2001). *Ecrits: A selection*. Translated by A. Sheridan. Routledge.

Lavalette, M., Ramsay, T., & Amara, M. (2018) 'From the river to the sea': Promoting Palestinian resistance through praxis. In N. Yu (ed.), *Consciousness-raising: Critical pedagogy and practice for social change* (pp. 135–151). Routledge.

Lear, J. (2005). *Freud*. Routledge.

Leland, D. (1988). Lacanian psychoanalysis and French feminism: Toward an adequate political psychology. *Hypatia*, 3(3), 81–103.

Lykes, M. B., & Moane, G. (2009). Editors' introduction: Whither feminist liberation psychology? Critical explorations of feminist and liberation psychologies for a globalizing world. *Feminism & Psychology*, 19(3), 283–297.

Malherbe, N. (2021). A psychopolitical interpretation of de-alienation: Marxism, psychoanalysis, and liberation psychology. *Psychoanalysis, Culture & Society*, 26 (3), 263–283.

Malm, A. (2023). *Fighting in a world on fire: The next generation's guide to protecting the climate and saving our future*. Verso.

Martín-Baró, I. (1994). *Writings for a liberation psychology*. Harvard University Press.

McCarthy, L., & Moon, J. (2018). Disrupting the gender institution: Consciousness-raising in the cocoa value chain. *Organization Studies*, 39(9), 1153–1177.

McGowan, T. (2013). *Enjoying what we don't have: The political project of psychoanalysis*. University of Nebraska Press.

Mirvis, P. (2008). Executive development through consciousness-raising experiences. *Academy of Management Learning & Education*, 7(2), 173–188.

Mitchell, J. (1971). *Women's estate*. Penguin.

Montero, M. (1994). Consciousness raising, conversion, and de-ideologization in community psychosocial work. *Journal of Community Psychology*, 22(1), 3–11.

Moodley, S. (ed.). (2018). *Time to remember: Reflections of women from the Black Consciousness Movement*. Women for Awareness.

Moraga, C, & Anzaldúa, G. (eds). (1983). *This bridge called my back: Writings by radical women of color*. Kitchen Table Press.

Nassi, A. J., & Abramowitz, S. I. (1978). Raising consciousness about women's groups: Process and outcome research. *Psychology of Women Quarterly*, 3(2), 139–156.

Olcott, J. (2017). *International women's year: The greatest consciousness-raising event in history*. Oxford University Press.

Parker, I. (2011). *Lacanian psychoanalysis: Revolutions in subjectivity*. Routledge.

Parker, I. & Pavón-Cuéllar, D. (2021). *Psychoanalysis and revolution: Critical psychology for liberation movements*. 1968 Press.

Pillow, W. (2003). Confession, catharsis, or cure? Rethinking the uses of reflexivity as methodological power in qualitative research. *International Journal of Qualitative Studies in Education*, 16(2), 175–196.

Pringle, R., & Thorpe, H. (2017). Theory and reflexivity. In M. L. Silk, D. L. Andrews, & H. Thorpe (eds), *Routledge handbook of physical cultural studies* (pp. 32–41). Routledge.

Redstockings Collective. (1970). How women are kept apart. In S. Stambler (ed.), *Women's liberation: Blueprint for the future* (pp. 23–38). Ace Books.

Reskin, B. (2005). Unconsciousness raising: The pernicious effects of unconscious bias. *Regional Review*, 1, 32–37.

Rosenthal, N. B. (1984). Consciousness raising: From revolution to re-evaluation. *Psychology of Women Quarterly*, 8(4), 309–326.

Ruck, N. (2015). Liberating minds: Consciousness-raising as a bridge between feminism and psychology in 1970s Canada. *History of Psychology*, 18(3), 297–311.

Rustin, M., & Armstrong, D. (2019). Psychoanalysis, social science and the Tavistock tradition. *Psychoanalysis, Culture & Society*, 24(4), 473–492.

Ruti, M. (2008). The fall of fantasies: A Lacanian reading of lack. *Journal of the American Psychoanalytic Association*, 56(2), 483–508.

Ryan, J., & Trevithick, P. A. (1988). Unconsciousness raising with working class women. In S. Krzowski & P. Land (Eds.), *Our experience: Workshops at the women's therapy centre* (pp. 63–83). Women's Press.

Sarachild, K. (1978). Consciousness-raising: A radical weapon. In K. Sarachild (ed.), *Feminist revolution* (pp. 144–150). Random House.

Sherriff, L. (2015). White students form human shield to protect Black #FeesMustFall protesters from South African police. *Huffington Post*. Retrieved from www.huffingtonpost.co.uk/2015/10/22/white-students-form-human-shield-protect-black-protesters-south-african-police_n_8356054.html.

Singh, A. A. (2016). Moving from affirmation to liberation in psychological practice with transgender and gender nonconforming clients. *American Psychologist*, 71(8), 755–762.

Southgate, J. (1983). How to run a Zenalys Group (or unconsciousness-raising group). *Self & Society*, 11(1), 25–32.

Sowards, S. K., & Renegar, V. R. (2004). The rhetorical functions of consciousness-raising in third wave feminism. *Communication Studies*, 55(4), 535–552.

Stavrakakis, Y. (2007). *The Lacanian left: Psychoanalysis, theory, politics*. Edinburgh University Press.

Stevens, G. (2023). (Un)consciousness-raising, (un)knowability, lack and spectrums of solidarity: Discussion of "unconsciousness-raising". *Psychoanalytic Dialogues*, 33 (4), 486–490.

Suffla, S., & Seedat, M. (2021). Africa's knowledge archives, Black Consciousness and reimagining community psychology. In G. Stevens & C. Sonn (eds), *Decoloniality, knowledge production and epistemic justice in contemporary community psychology* (pp. 21–38). Springer.

Suffla, S., Seedat, M., & Bawa, U. (2015). Reflexivity as enactment of critical community psychologies: Dilemmas of voice and positionality in a multi-country photovoice study. *Journal of Community Psychology*, 43(1), 9–21.

Tupinambá, G. (2021). *The desire of psychoanalysis: exercises in Lacanian thinking*. Northwestern University Press.

Weitz, R. (1982). Feminist consciousness raising, self-concept, and depression. *Sex Roles*, 8(3), 231–241.

Winship, G. (2005). Consciousness-raising and well-being in public sphere organizations: A historical review of psychoanalytical approaches. *Psychoanalytic Psychotherapy*, 19(3), 233–245.

Woods, A. (2023). Discussion: "Unconsciousness-raising". *Psychoanalytic Dialogues*, 33(4), 475–485.

Yu, N. (ed.). (2018). *Consciousness-raising: Critical pedagogy and practice for social change*. Routledge.

Chapter 5

Memory Otherwise

Introduction

In her study on slavery in the Cape, Gqola (2010) refers to *unremembering* as a calculated mode of historiographic erasure that marks dominant memory work. More often than not, it is the riotous histories of expropriated labours, lands, and lives that go unremembered (see Rodney, 1972). Struggle itself tends to go largely unremembered. James (1994, p. 77), for example, notes that the only place we do not find twentieth-century Black-led struggles for decolonisation are "in the pages of capitalist historians". Unremembering ensures that the colonised are read through the terms set by Euro-modernity and are thus unable to emerge as historical subjects when they refuse these terms (Rifkin, 2017). As Fanon (1963, p. 201) put it, it is by "a kind of perverted logic" that colonial capitalism "turns to the past of the oppressed people, and distorts, disfigures, and destroys it."

It seems clear that psychoanalytic liberation psychology practitioners would reject such colonial historiographic approaches. How, then, might we go about approaching memory work within and for an anti-capitalist project? Some have posited that we can analyse colonial capitalist history via what Freud (1896, p. 169) spoke of as "the return of the repressed memories", wherein we repeat actions in the present in lieu of remembering that which is too traumatic to bring into conscious memory. Karatani (2011), for instance, reads capitalism as a kind of structural repetition, where systemic exploitation, dispossession, and expropriation repeat over time. As useful as Karatani's approach and others like it may be, such an approach risks imposing a reductive, linear timescale of breaks and resumptions onto capitalist history. It is more generative, I believe, to follow Samudzi (2021), who demonstrates that capitalism's genocidal history is not a series of repetitions precisely because this history has continued along the trajectory it has always been on. The violent forms of capitalist accumulation may have changed over time, but violent accumulation as such has never ceased under capitalism. Take South Africa, for example. Gobodo-Madikizela (2023) notes that the 1946 African Mine Workers Strike, the 1960 Sharpeville Massacre, the 1976

DOI: 10.4324/9781003612728-5

Soweto Uprising, the 2011 murder of Andries Tatane (who was participating in a service delivery protest), and the 2013 Marikana Massacre are all outcomes of a racial capitalist structure operating across different epochs. It is because, as Wolpe (1990) writes, capitalism represents "diversity and discontinuity within a process of continuity" (p. 8) that it requires an "analysis of discontinuities within continuity" (p. 61). Samudzi (2021) goes on to argue that it is against capital's continuing – rather than repeated – structures of accumulation that memory operates not as mere recollection, but as archives which exist in our bodies and affective responses to the present. How we recall these archives within the continuing structures of capital accumulation – within these temporal modes of non-change – has psychic implications (see Hook, 2015). Psychoanalytic liberation psychology is well placed to engage these implications in and for anti-capitalist movements.

In this chapter, I argue that anti-capitalism's memory project is one that looks beyond official, neatly linear historiography, and towards fragments of memory that allow the individuals who constitute a collective to feel into past struggles and connect affectively as comrades working in a lineage of struggle. I am, here, concerned with memory otherwise, which is to say, how we might recall the past in ways that are non-synchronous with capitalist impositions of time (see Bloch, 1986; Paris, 2025). Psychoanalytic liberation psychology is able to engage with memory otherwise precisely because, unlike mainstream iterations of psychology and psychoanalysis (Thabolwethu & Makama, 2025), it is concerned less with the facticity of memory than it is with the subjective truth of it (see Leader, 2008).

In what follows, I discuss politicising memory in and against capitalist conceptions of time, after which I attempt to delineate the role of psychoanalytic liberation psychology in relation to politicised memory. Here, I focus specifically on reconstituting re-membering (a memory practice that has been developed within the liberation psychology paradigm) through psychoanalytic insights. Following this, I reflect on my work with anti-capitalist movements in the south of Johannesburg, where activists have drawn on several conflicting temporalities and memory fragments to re-member their community as well as the struggles to defend their community against the onslaughts of capital.

Politicising Memory

The recollection of history is undoubtedly a political undertaking (Paret, 2018a), but it is not in and of itself an anti-capitalist one. Memory can and often does serve reactionary purposes. Eagleton (1996, p. 33) warns us:

> For a whole lineage of liberal or rightwing thinkers, a sensitive attunement to historical context, to the cultural mouldings of the self, to the subliminal voice of tradition and the force of the local or idiosyncratic,

has been a way of discrediting what they take to be the anaemic ahistorical rationality of the radicals.

There are those who remember in order to recapture real or imagined gratifications from idealised histories of oppression (Boym, 2007; Jameson, 1974). In our time, we have seen Trump accrue considerable political power under the auspices of *Make America Great Again*; Bolsonaro gaining much support by aligning with twentieth-century fascistic Brazilian integralism; and white nationalists in South Africa expressing intense nostalgia for apartheid rule. Paradoxically, memory can also form part of unremembering. Contemporary memory culture in Germany has, for example, leveraged memories of the horrors perpetuated by Nazism to consolidate present-day relations with Israel's genocidal apartheid regime, all while ignoring the enormous violence that characterised Germany's twentieth-century colonial project, which included the Herero and Nama genocide in Namibia (Mishra, 2025).

Even when memory work is undertaken by avowed anti-capitalists, this work is not in every instance politically generative. To dwell on the memory of struggle can, in some instances, take us away from the struggles happening around us. There are anti-capitalist radicals who, when faced with repeated political defeat, are no longer able to enter into the living tradition of anti-capitalist struggle, relegating such struggle to the "realm of memory" (Traverso, 2017, p. 97). The anti-capitalist future for which we fight thus becomes confined to the memory of a time when such a future seemed possible (Delanty, 2024). Consequently, Brown (1999, p. 26) argues, the anti-capitalist Left risks becoming

> more attached to its impossibility than to its potential fruitfulness, a Left that is most at home dwelling not in hopefulness but in its own marginality and failure, a Left that is thus caught in a structure of melancholic attachment to a certain strain of its own dead past, whose spirit is ghostly, whose structure of desire is backward looking and punishing.

In light of all of this, it would appear that situating memory within anti-capitalist resistance efforts depends less on the particular content of our memories than on how we bring these memories to bear on the present. Remembering struggle, or rather remembering within and for struggle, can function as "a work of documentation, repair and reparation" (Gana, 2023, p. 14), and it can reinvigorate the temporalities of struggle (i.e. our psychic experience of time in struggle; Hook, 2015) in ways that inform increasingly disallowed attempts to think and act upon an anti-capitalist future (White, 2024).

Memories of struggle can infuse today's struggles with a kind of psychic urgency that recalls the lineage within which resistance operates. As such, memory functions to negate the present and to project the future for which we fight by holding up images of the past which serve as political and hermeneutic points of contact from which to obtain revolutionary energies during times of stagnation and defeat (Jameson, 1974). As Pavón-Cuéllar (2017, p. 39) writes: "We think with our history, and feel through it." And as Sultana (2022, p. 10) insists:

> [We] feel sorrow for a past that never got to be, a present that is incomplete, unknowables that haunt and pique. Our memories are reshaped and respond to local and global forces, we are all different but we share some common histories. These are the fertile grounds where colonial and imperial wounds and resultant rage, grief, and desire are not minimized but recognized as part of the driving forces of resurgence and liberation.

The task of anti-capitalism today is one of completing the struggles of the past, of finishing the task of liberation in our time (Bloch, 1986). We can refuse capitalism's teleological claim on inevitability by remembering, however partially, history otherwise. This is intensely psycho-political work, and it is work with which psychoanalytic liberation psychology must concern itself.

Psychoanalytic Liberation Psychology and the Politicisation of Memory

Dominant conceptions of psychology and psychoanalysis tend to confine memory to the "future-oriented individualism" that marks capitalist ideology (Schmitt et al., 2021, p. 406). As such, both disciplines have given relatively little attention to how the historical forces of capital accumulation shape our capacity to remember. Martín-Baró (1994, p. 30), for instance, wrote that mainstream psychology insists on a "permanent psychological present" which inadequately attends to the flows of history in, against, and beneath which the subject remembers. Much of psychoanalysis has similarly overinvested in temporalities of whiteness, wherein the translatability and legibility of memory are confined to colonial logics of accumulation, erasure, and dispossession (Sheehi, 2022).

To understand how practitioners working in the psychoanalytic liberation psychology paradigm might approach memory work, we must first outline some of the ways by which liberation psychology and psychoanalysis have, respectively, approached memory. Let us begin with liberation psychology. A central task of liberation psychology, Martín-Baró (1994, p. 30) wrote, is that of recovering historical memory, a process which "supposes the reconstruction of models of identification that, instead of chaining and caging the people, open up the horizon for them, toward their liberation and fulfilment". Underlying this process is an emphasis on collective representations of history that open up new ways of knowing the world and acting in it (Adams & Kurtiş, 2012). Although there are several ways by which liberation psychology practitioners have sought to recover historical memory, re-membering represents an appropriately broad, community-oriented means of doing so. We can understand re-membering as an approach to building, excavating, and consolidating history by engaging critically with the pasts that have been dismembered – or unremembered (Gqola, 2010) – by capital-ism (Adams & Kurtiş, 2012; Lykes & McGillen, 2021; Malherbe, 2020). As Bhabha (1994, p. 215) describes it: "Remembering is never a quiet act of introspection or retrospection. It is a painful re-membering, a putting toge-ther of the dismembered past to make sense of the trauma of the present." The re-membering process is not singularly constituted. It operates as a contextually embedded map that guides the focus of memory work as well as the political purposes to which this work is put. For instance, where those working in the liberation psychology paradigm in Latin America have sought to re-member the past via testimonios (see Cervantes et al., 2021; Fernández, 2022), liberation psychology practitioners in South Africa have attempted to do so through unofficial and neglected archives (see Malherbe & Canham, 2024; Seedat & Suffla, 2017; Stevens et al., 2013). The goal here is not to develop a complete picture of history, but to excavate the memory fragments of a dismembered past which hold psychic resonance for those involved in contemporary anti-capitalist struggle.

Moving on to the memory project of psychoanalysis, Hobsbawm (2011, p. 244) comments that "I don't think histories have an awful lot to learn from Freud, who was a bad historian, whenever he wrote anything about history". We should be clear, then, that psychoanalysis is concerned with memory, not history. Such a concern is, however, less about what we remember than it is about how we remember. Psychoanalysts pay attention to the role of trauma, psychic defences, resistance, and repression in configuring our memories. In this, psychoanalysts endeavour to carve out a space for people to apprehend the past through its psychic affects (Jameson, 1974), thereby revealing the present conditions that determine how the past is narrated and in which the past is preserved (Truscott & Hook, 2014). Freud (1920) found that people do not remember traumatic incidents directly. They tend to do so via (usually unwanted) repeated action. It is because we are unable to directly recall what we have repressed that we act it out; compelled to repeat the traumas that we cannot master (Lear, 2005). Thus, for psychoanalysis, the past exists beyond what we can recall, in the shape of our psychological engagements with and investments in history (Pavón-Cuéllar, 2017). Put differently, psychoanalysis is attuned to the ways by which forgetting forms part of memory, taking seriously the anxieties and psychic investments that constitute this forgetting-remembering dialectic (see Rose, 2011). We are, therefore, bound together not only in our repetitions, but also in our incapacity to summon the totality of our past experiences (see Parker & Pavón-Cuéllar, 2021).

In considering how memory has been approached within both liberation psychology and psychoanalysis, we are led to ask how we might practise re-membering through the insights of psychoanalysis, which is to say, how we can approach memory work from within psychoanalytic liberation psychology. A psychoanalytic conception of re-membering, I want to argue, insists on our being non-synchronous with capital's imperial temporalities of endless productivity, immediate possession, unending dispossession, and eternal extraction (see Rifkin, 2017; Thabolwethu & Makama, 2025). To re-member through our non-synchronicity is to take heed of and disrupt contemporary historiographic processes of invisibilisation and inferiorisation. As Sheehi (2022, p. 607) writes: "In a liberatory psychoanalytic praxis, this is where our technical and psychic energetic pull should live – not in the ghost of the past, but in the monadic material being before us".

Moving towards non-synchronicity asks that the re-membering process permit within our memories timescales that may not be compatible with one another à la psychoanalysis (see Hartocollis, 2003). Here, we allow for a kind of psychic retroactivity, or what Freud called Nachträglichkeit (see Hollander, 2018), wherein the meaning of the past is constituted by its activation in the present which, in turn, foregrounds the future into which we want to direct history (Gobodo-Madikizela, 2023; Hook, 2015). The future, in other words, is located in our present-day disruptions of the past. When re-membering is attuned to Nachträglichkeit, it calls on an intensive engagement not only with how capitalism distributes trauma along racialised, gendered, and class lines, but also with how struggle ensures that emancipatory futures are not relegated to the past.

To re-member against capitalist temporalities, to embrace non-synchronicity, is to allow a breaking through of the psychic energies that have been disallowed within official historiographies (such as anger, unsettlement, rage, resentment, hate), offering to us new foundations for feeling into historical processes of dismemberment (see Hook, 2013). Excavating affect in this manner can serve as a psychic basis for connecting with comrades across space; facilitating a *feeling with* those whom we struggle alongside. The excavation of affect also allows us to connect with comrades across time: those who were engaged in anti-capitalist struggles of the past, struggles which do not repeat, but continue into today. As Benjamin (2007) writes, our struggles may well be "nourished by the image of enslaved ancestors rather than that of liberated grandchildren" (p. 260). Re-membering thus resembles hooks's (2009) insistence that we travel to those memories which have not been recorded so that we can disrupt a present whose social ordering has disallowed such memories from speaking.

Re-membering, as I am describing it here, does not hold gaps and contradictions apart from memory (see Worby & Ally, 2013). The affects that encircle our attempts to grasp the past do not emerge through a fully formed picture of history, but through disparate historical fragments. Such fragmentation can take the form of specific, disjointed recollections of the past (see Malherbe, 2020), as well as the heirlooms, trinkets, and knick-knacks that honour and feel into the past in ways that cohere with non-synchronous temporal experience (Benjamin, 2008). To reconstruct the past through fragments makes clear that history is open to rearrangement, with different fragments overlapping and interrupting each other, moving across different timescales (see Eagleton, 1996). It is with fragments that we are able to symbolise our experience of history in different ways; making room for repressed memories and psychic blockages to emerge in and between fragments (see Lau, 2021; Leader, 2008). For psychoanalytic liberation psychology praxis, constituting history through memory fragments requires abandoning the capitalist injunction to exert mastery over the past (see Gqola, 2010), while also recognising the anxieties that can accompany attempts to engage with the past without the promise of mastery (see Fields & Fields, 2022).

Benjamin (1986) argues that if labour strikes interrupt capitalist time, so too can attempts to recall time via historic fragmentation. Both modes of temporal interruption can act alongside or through one another to make way for anti-capitalist temporalities. To re-member within anti-capitalist movements is to resist the temporalities imposed by political defeat, that is, the experience of defeat as the unalterable destiny of those to whom capital has sought to structurally prohibit historical agency (see Gana, 2023). Re-membering the past is thus not only about attaining practical lessons in political strategy and tactics – though it is surely this too – but it is also an attempt to reject the temporal foreclosure of struggle by investing psychically in struggle's non-synchronicity (see Sheehi, 2022). Barakat (2021), for instance, notes that in Palestine, ongoing struggles against Israeli settler violence hold within them memories and temporal experiences which are, for many Palestinians, a necessity of survival. Becoming non-synchronous with temporalities of eternal defeat, we might then say, asks that we move towards becoming simultaneous with one another in contexts of enduring struggle (see Paris, 2025), thereby turning capital's "*compulsive* reenactment of aggressivity" against itself, "into a *compulsory* act of insurrection" (Gana, 2023, p. 21).

Today's anti-capitalist memory movements operate through a range of solidarity networks that make clear the interconnections of struggle (see Escobar, 2022). For example, on the so-called Separation Wall that runs through the West Bank, we find memorials to Palestinians murdered by the Israeli state alongside memorials of George Floyd, who was murdered by US police forces in 2020 (Patel, 2020). To re-member in these ways is to insist on the global purview of capitalism, and to attune anti-capitalism to a necessarily internationalist orientation. It is also to confront capital's globalised processes of unremembering (see Gqola, 2010). As Adams & Kurtiş (2012, p. 20) explain: "forgetting and silence are deliberate practices of remembering and communicating that people actively deploy (whether as a conscious individual strategy or culturally evolved technologies) to manage or contain problematic past events". Psychoanalytic liberation psychology praxis must, accordingly, endeavour to work with activists to create space for re-member-ing and refusing the erasure of those whose desires, freedom, actions, and lives go unremembered within capitalism's necropolitical regimes of accumu-lation (see Escobar, 2022; Traverso, 2017). In this way, re-membering can become a life-affirming practice (see Sheehi & Sheehi, 2024), one that is real (rather than correct or incorrect), and one that is animated by the utopian temporalities of the future which run alongside desires to overcome what is lacking in the capitalist present (see Delanty, 2024; Paris, 2025).

Re-membering is intensely agonistic precisely because people suffer from their memories, just as they suffer from not remembering them. To re-member is to risk re-traumatisation, and it is to ask uncomfortable questions about complicity in capitalist oppression (Malherbe, 2020). It is also to confront those invested in unremembering who seek to turn our gaze towards some pasts at the expense of others, and who seek to fix trauma in time, rendering it legible only through capital's colonial temporalities (Sheehi & Sheehi, 2024). In recognising the agonisms that mark memory work, we can begin the work of reflecting on the repetitions and continuations of historical pain as well as attachments to and investments in such pain, thus moving us towards envisioning a world which reckons with pain rather than builds societies on it (Hook, 2013). As Eagleton (1996, p. 35) writes, that people "are able, within limits, to make something of what makes them, is the very index of their historicity, a mode of being possible only to a labouring, linguistic creature."

To re-member is not to project present-day anti-capitalist desire into the past (Hobsbawm, 2011), but rather to understand anti-capitalism as an ongoing tradition that spans across capitalism's uneven geographies, modes of accumulation, and timescales. Indeed, we do not re-member to return to a romanticised past (Mamdani, 2020), but to begin the work of recalling the past from the perspective of those who have failed by and been expelled from the temporal standards set by capitalist modernity (Rees, 2021). Re-membering insists on the impermanence of capital's grip over temporality. As Fanon (1986 [1967], p. 179) so powerfully contends:

> I am not a prisoner of history. I should not seek there for the meaning of my destiny. I should constantly remind myself that the real leap consists in introducing invention into existence. In the world through which I travel, I am endlessly creating myself. I am a part of Being to the degree that I go beyond it.

Case Reflection

Much of the memory work undertaken in post-1994 South Africa has approached history through an individualising lens. The Truth and Reconci-liation Committee (TRC) hearings were exemplary in this respect. Taking place between 1996 and 1998, the TRC assumed a "'victim-centred' approach" (Gobodo-Madikizela, 2023, p. 68), wherein a criminal justice framework was employed to identify which individuals were responsible for which apartheid crimes. Important as the TRC undoubtedly was, it grappled insufficiently with how apartheid's structures functioned as a continuation of colonial capital (Mamdani, 2020). Systemic land dispossession and the hyper-exploitation of Black labour did not, for instance, assume a prominent place in the TRC proceedings (Ngcukaitobi, 2021). Indeed, even if recording and reflecting on history are indispensable for apprehending the past, these processes do not in and of themselves discontinue the structures of history (Berlant, 2008).

There is, however, a critical tradition of memory work in South Africa, a tradition that centres not only the continuing capitalist structures of history, but also the lineages of collective struggle directed against these structures. Some of this work, I maintain, is situated in psychoanalytic liberation psychology. For example, those involved in the Apartheid Archive Project have drawn from both psychological and psychoanalytic insights to analyse the stories that people tell of their experiences of apartheid, locating these stories simultaneously in history and in the present conjuncture (see Stevens et al., 2013). South Africans have also taken up psychology and psychoanalysis to revisit the TRC archives (e.g. Gobodo-Madikizela, 2023), read the unofficial archives of anti-capitalist community practitioners (e.g. Malherbe & Canham, 2024), and interpret overlooked knowledge archives in the Global South (e.g. Seedat & Suffla, 2017). Moreover, drawing on Dlamini's (2009) influential work, there has been a growth of nostalgia studies in the country, where psychoanalysis and – albeit to a lesser extent – psychology have been used for different analytic purposes (see e.g. Hook, 2015; Paret, 2018a; Worby & Ally, 2013). It is within this broad tradition of critical psycho-political memory work that I have sought to situate my own re-membering praxis, to which I will now turn.

Although land-based struggles in South Africa vary, they are in large part driven by the demand for sovereignty and ownership over the land from which impoverished Black South Africans and their ancestors have been dispossessed (Ngcukaitobi, 2021). These are struggles to own land beyond market-oriented sectional title logic, and they are struggles to develop land through sustainable agriculture, affordable housing, sanitation, reliable electricity, clean water, and community-directed programmes. These are also struggles, I want to argue, that re-member the past by demanding a break from the colonial capitalist order through which today's racial capitalist structures endure (Alexander, 2013). Contemporary land struggles in South Africa are, in other words, fundamentally struggles to re-member that which cannot find expression in a capitalist social order that hinges progress on dispossession. As we will see, the re-membering apparatuses of these land-based struggles open up subjectivities, identifications, and desires that transcend the pseudo-segregations that capital sets up between land and people.

The South African land activists with whom I have worked are based in the south of Johannesburg. There are well over fifty communities in this area for whom land-based dispossession has been central to their marginalisation. These histories of dispossession and, importantly, the struggles against dispossession, have gone largely undocumented. When these communities enter into public consciousness, they tend to do so via media reporting which focuses almost exclusively on how activists from these communities have interrupted the flows of capital with, for instance, highway protests that cause disruption to traffic and, in some instances, damage to property (Malherbe et al., 2021). In addition to obscuring the structures of oppression and lineages of struggle operative in these communities, such media reporting tends to confine the origins of these communities to static time signatures (e.g. *pre- apartheid; post-apartheid; the 1980s*) that are divorced from the structural mechanisms of land dispossession which have, in South Africa, operated across colonial time. We need not, however, rely on historiographies imposed from above to read and consolidate the land-based struggles taking place in the south of Johannesburg. Indeed, within the community-led movements waging these struggles, we encounter intensely affective re-membering practices. Songs and martyrs from the anti-apartheid era, lineages of prefigurative action, mourning past defeats, and celebrating historic victories all form part of the organisational infrastructure of these movements. And as we will see, by shifting between non-synchronous temporalities, these movements make available images of a future unmoored from the structurally violent timescales of capital.

Let us look at one of the communities undertaking land-based struggle in the south of Johannesburg. In early 2020, large numbers of people began to set up shack settlements in this community. The South African Police Service was swiftly deployed to tear down these settlements, doing so on dubious charges of illegality. Anti-capitalist forces in the community quickly mobilised. Through a combination of militant organisation (which saw community members defending themselves directly from police attacks while also conducting a series of highway protests) and legal contestation (wherein a case against the police evictions was fought in court), the community eventually won the right to settlement. Walking through the community today, one finds shops, subsistence farms, clean energy and recycling initiatives, and creches. Residents have also established a number of small parks throughout their community. Anti-capitalist activism remains alive and well in this community and forms a central part of its identity. Activists have taken to naming streets in the community after political values and ideals of struggle (*freedom; liberation; peace*). Nonetheless, the community occupies a precarious social position. There has been almost no in situ development, with the South African state refusing to provide water, sanitation, housing, or electricity infrastructure.

After activists won the right to settle, several colleagues and I began working with social movement actors in this community to produce a documentary film that sought to re-member the community through struggles over land. The film, which featured community members explaining the land-based struggles with which they have been involved, was later screened in several locations in and beyond the community. The point of the film, community members made clear, is not simply to capture and communicate land-based struggles from the perspective of those involved in these struggles, but to symbolise the non-synchronous formations of struggle. Land, not time, was thus to structure how community members recalled and felt into the past.

During the preproduction phases of the documentary, community members rejected what Jameson (1974, p. 130) refers to as "past-oriented time", where the meaning and value of contemporary struggle is drawn exclusively from the past. They stressed that the film must foreground today's most pertinent struggles. Past struggles, they insisted, should be represented in the documentary only insofar as they frame the present. The film must not function as boutique historical inquiry, they contended. We might, here, recall Marx (2000 [1852], p. 330), who writes that those anti-capitalists who awaken the dead do so for "the purpose of glorifying the new struggles, not of parodying the old; of magnifying the given tasks in imagination, not of taking flight from their solution in reality; of finding once more the spirit of revolution, not of making its ghost walk again".

For these community activists, history could be accessed most viscerally through the recollections of the past that are operative in present-day struggles for land. Stated differently, we retrieve the spirit of South Africa's history, rather than its facticity, in the landed struggles of today which serve as continuations of struggles against slavery, colonialism, and apartheid. Community members insisted that theirs were "struggles after liberation" – struggles which ask us to return to how we understand and have hitherto signified liberation in post-1994 South Africa.

In the documentary, community struggles were represented, in Paret's (2018b, p. 354) words, as being less about returning to a singular imagined past, than they are "about an absent future" – one whose promises have not yet been realised. As Gobodo-Madikizela (2023, p. 72) writes: "What is unfinished does not return as a ghostly, phantomatic presence but rather as a real absence for which someone must be answerable." As such, today's land-based struggles do not signify past political failure as much as they constitute what Traverso (2017) calls future-oriented memory: operational memory practices that seek to redirect the course of history.

We see in the documentary that early 2020 marks the moment when the South African state could no longer ignore this community. And thus, it is this moment that tends to be taken as the community's origin point by South Africa's elite political and media classes. It is, however, immediately clear when talking to community members – one of whom was, at the time I spoke to him, in his late 90s – that the community is, in fact, much older than this.

Black people have been making community on this land since the early 1900s, before white settlers arrived. Later, in the 1970s, when the apartheid state prevented Black South Africans from owning land, increasing numbers of families began to settle in the community. In the documentary, community members draw on each of these three origin points (early 1900s, 1970s, and 2020) to historicise their community. Together, these long and short histories make available expansive, non-linear ways by which to inhabit time, land, and the traumas locked into land-based dispossession (see Thabolwethu & Makama, 2025). These are "multiple histories that are grounded in community" (ka Canham, 2023, p. 12) which can be drawn on to articulate the different relations to the land – affective, epistemic, political, and health-related – that community members pass through each day.

In the documentary, people re-membered their community's landed history through fragments. These fragments were, in some cases, disjointed, largely variable accounts pieced together by different generations, wherein the affective swirls surrounding land were prioritised over narrative singularity. In other cases, people drew on physical memory fragments, such as deeds that promised but never delivered state housing. These fragments survive historic dismemberment. They do not represent histories of militant resistance. Instead, they form part of the historic struggle to live with dignity. It is, therefore, through the non-synchronous, affectively charged fragments that surround dispossession that struggles against such dispossession were articulated in the documentary. Indeed, it was with these fragments that people felt into their past so as to bring renewed intensity to today's anti-capitalist struggles for land.

Constructing a filmic narrative with historical fragments of land-based struggle served as a naked declaration of the documentary's historiographic gaps. At public screenings of the documentary, audiences proceeded to fill these gaps with the kinds of affective expression that tend to go unexpressed in the linear histographies which make a fetish of wholly coherent, recognisable images of history. As such, audience members connected with one another through the non-synchronous time registers that were made available in the documentary. At different screenings, people sobbed, sang, and raged, sharing and re-signifying traumas (their own and those of others) in light of present-day struggles. The materiality of history was not, of course, repressed at these screenings. Rather, the material character of history was activated psychically in order to bind together the collective into what Alexander (2013, p. 130) calls the "new historical community", wherein oppressive and divisive identifications that sever human connection and internalise colonial logic cannot thrive. It is precisely because the new historical community is not a singular, entirely cohesive, or without agonism that it enables the affective, non-synchronous character of the past to breathe.

It is important that anti-capitalist struggles not be equated with the struggle to remember differently. Adams and Kurtiş (2012) have demonstrated that an excessive focus on memory within community struggle can draw attention away from the capitalist structures acting onto communities. In the south of Johannesburg, this has never been the case. Re-membering has always formed part of land-based struggles, rather than operating as struggle itself, and – as was repeatedly observed at different community screenings of the documentary film – memories of struggle in one community were connected to the memories of those living in other marginalised communities who share in South Africa's history of racist violence and land dispossession. Memory was, therefore, not articulated otherwise for its own sake, but as an affective foundation for building inter-community solidarity.

Hartocollis (2003) warns against psychoanalysts defying the temporal boundaries that have been agreed upon with analysts. This may include missing sessions, as well as arriving late or too early for a session. To commit to these temporal boundaries is, of course, to adhere in some respects to capitalism's imposition of time, where time's value is measured in relation to the surplus extracted from it. The boundaries of time cannot be transgressed without consequence under capitalism. In the fight to constitute time and memory differently – the fight to re-member – psychoanalytic liberation psychology cannot adhere to such capitalist conceptions of time. In occupied Palestine, for example, Sheehi and Sheehi (2022) recount that Palestinian clinicians are attuned to how Palestinian analysands are subject to the settler timescales produced by Zionist colonial technologies – such as checkpoints, blockades, walls, and prisons – which manage, monitor, control, and even cease the mobility of Palestinians.

During the production and screening of the documentary film, there were instances when community members did not arrive at the agreed-upon time or day. This was due to reasons ranging from unforeseen political matters, such as the arrest of comrades, or housing/land documents that needed to be submitted at the local magistrate court. On some days, people were too exhausted to participate. Psychoanalytic liberation psychology practice must attune itself to these oppressive experiences of time precisely because such experiences point to the capitalist future from which we seek to turn away, a future where the extremes and the traumas of the past can, at best, only ever be managed in the present (White, 2024). As the Readsura Decolonial Editorial Collective (2022, p. 272) write with respect to how psychology might form part of decolonial land-based praxis:

> the point of an emphasis on de/coloniality with respect to ways of knowing and being is not to dilute struggles for land and justice or to rescue settler futurity, but instead to mobilize even stronger responses to them by affording imagination and realization of futures delinked from modernity/coloniality.

The struggle to re-member is fundamental to imagining and realising such futures.

Conclusion

The task of re-membering is to feel into history without the burden of narrative coherence or provable facticity. To re-member is to foreground and build psychic fidelity to the non-synchronicity of struggle. And while those who re-member do not need the psy-disciplines (and the fidelity of these disciplines to capitalist time), I hope to have made a case for how psychoanalytic liberation psychology can contribute to the re-membering process in politically generative ways.

The gaps of my own memory are undoubtedly operative in the recollections that appear in this chapter. It should not be assumed that my case reflection is entirely accurate, impartial, complete, or even shared by everyone present at the events described. It is my hope that future work within psychoanalytic liberation psychology approaches the re-membering process in more collective and creative ways than I have here. A plurality of forms and voices need not dilute or depoliticise memory work, but can instead stretch and embolden the anti-capitalist ambitions of constituting memory otherwise.

References

Adams, G., & Kurtiş, T. (2012). Collective memory practices as tools for reconciliation: Perspectives from liberation and cultural psychology. *African Conflict and Peacebuilding Review*, 2(2), 5–28.

Alexander, N. (2013). *Thoughts on the new South Africa*. Jacana.

Barakat, R. (2021). "Ramadan does not come for free": Refusal as new and ongoing in Palestine. *Journal of Palestine Studies*, 50(4), 90–95.

Benjamin, W. (1986). *Reflections: Essays, aphorisms, autobiographical writings*. Schocken Books.

Benjamin, W. (2007). *Illuminations: Essays and reflections*. Random House.

Benjamin, W. (2008). *The work of art in the age of technological reproducibility and other writings on media*. Harvard University Press.

Berlant, L. (2008). Thinking about feeling historical. *Emotion, Space and Society*, 1, 4–9.

Bhabha, H. (1994). *The location of culture*. Routledge.

Bloch, E. (1986). *The principle of hope*. Blackwell.

Boym, S. (2007). Nostalgia and its discontents. *Hedgehog Review*, 9(2), 7–18.

Brown, W. (1999). Resisting left melancholy. *Boundary 2*, 26(3), 19–27.

Cervantes, A., Flores Carmona, J., & Torres Fernández, I. (2021). Testimonios and liberation psychology as praxis: Informing educators in the borderlands. *Journal of Latinos and Education*, 20(1), 20–31.

Delanty, G. (2024). Introduction: Social theory and the idea of the future. *European Journal of Social Theory*, 27(2), 153–173.

Dlamini, J. (2009). *Native nostalgia*. Jacana Media.

Eagleton, T. (1996). *The illusions of postmodernism*. Blackwell Publishing.

Escobar, J. (2022). The role of memory practices in building spiritual solidarity for survivors of state violence. *American Journal of Community Psychology*, 69(3–4), 403–414.

Fanon, F. (1963). *The wretched of the earth*. Grove.

Fanon, F. (1986 [1967]). *Black skin, white masks*. Pluto.

Fernández, J. S. (2022). A mujerista liberation psychology perspective on testimonio to cultivate decolonial healing. *Women & Therapy*, 45(2–3), 131–156.

Fields, B. J., & Fields, K. E. (2022). *Racecraft: The soul of inequality in American life*. Verso.

Freud, S. (1896). Further remarks on the neuropsychoses of defence. In J. Strachey (ed., trans.), *The standard edition of the complete psychological works of Sigmund Freud, vol. 3*. Hogarth Press.

Freud, S. (1920). Beyond the pleasure principle. In J. Strachey (ed., trans.), *The standard edition of the complete psychological works of Sigmund Freud, vol. 18*. Hogarth Press.

Gana, N. (2023). *Melancholy acts: Defeat and cultural critique in the Arab world*. Fordham University Press.

Gobodo-Madikizela, P. (2023). The afterlife of apartheid: A triadic temporality of trauma. *Social Dynamics*, 49(1), 67–86.

Gqola, P. D. (2010). *What is slavery to me?* Wits University Press.

Hartocollis, P. (2003). Time and the psychoanalytic situation. *The Psychoanalytic Quarterly*, 72(4), 939–957.

Hobsbawm, E. (2011). *On history*. Hachette.

Hollander, N. (2018). Psychoanalysts bearing witness: Trauma and memory in Latin America. In P. Gherovici & C. Christian (eds), *Psychoanalysis in the barrios: Race, class, and the unconscious* (pp. 38–53). Routledge.

Hook, D. (2013). *(Post)apartheid conditions: Psychoanalysis and social formation*. Springer.

Hook, D. (2015). Petrified life. *Social Dynamics*, 41(3), 438–460.

hooks, b. (2009). *Belonging: A culture of place*. Routledge.

James, C. L. R. (1994). *C.L.R. James and revolutionary Marxism: Selected writings of C.L.R. James 1939–1949*. Prometheus Books.

Jameson, F. (1974). *Marxism and form: Twentieth-century dialectical theories of literature*. Princeton University Press.

ka Canham, H. (2023). *Riotous deathscapes*. Duke University Press.

Karatani, K. (2011). *History and repetition*. Columbia University Press.

Kessi, S., Boonzaier, F., & Gekeler, B. S. (2021). *Pan-Africanism and psychology in decolonial times*. Palgrave Macmillan.

Lau, U. (2021). Between Fanon and Lacan: Rupturing spaces for the return of the oppressed. *Studies in Gender and Sexuality*, 22(4), 278–292.

Leader, D. (2008). *The new black: Mourning, melancholia and depression*. Penguin.

Lear, J. (2005). *Freud*. Routledge.

Lykes, M. B., & McGillen, G. G. (2021). Re/membering Ignacio Martín-Baró: Provocations and insights towards liberating psychology in the twenty-first century. In G. Stevens & C. C. Sonn (eds), *Decoloniality and epistemic justice in contemporary community psychology* (pp. 79–99). Springer.

Malherbe, N. (2020). Articulating liberation psychologies of culture. *Journal of Theoretical and Philosophical Psychology*, 40(4), 203–218.

Malherbe, N., & Canham, H. (2024). Reading a liberation psychology archive in South Africa. *South African Journal of Psychology*, 54(4), 475–487.

Malherbe, N., Seedat, M., & Suffla, S. (2021). Analyzing discursive constructions of community in newspaper articles. *American Journal of Community Psychology*, 67 (3–4), 433–446.

Malherbe, N., Stevens, G., & Suffla, S. (2023). Psychanalyse, sociogenie, et condition post-apartheid en Afrique Du Sud. In S. Mendelsohn & L. Boni (eds), *Psychanalyse du Reste du Monde: Géo-Histoire d'une Subversion* (pp. 503–523). La Découverte.

Mamdani, M. (2020). *Neither settler nor native: The making and unmaking of permanent minorities*. Harvard University Press.

Martín-Baró, I. (1994). *Writings for a liberation psychology*:Harvard University Press.

Marx, K. (2000 [1852]). Eighteenth Brumaire of Louis Bonaparte. In D. McLellan (ed.), *Selected writings*, 2nd edition (pp. 329–355). Oxford University Press.

Mishra, P. (2025). Israel and the delusions of Germany's 'memory culture'. *The Guardian*, retrieved from www.theguardian.com/news/2025/jan/30/israel-and-the-de lusions-of-germanys-memory-culture.

Ngcukaitobi, T. (2021). *Land matters: South Africa's failed land reforms and the road ahead*. Random House.

Paret, M. (2018a). Critical nostalgias in democratic South Africa. *The Sociological Quarterly*, 59(4), 678–696.

Paret, M. (2018b). The politics of local resistance in urban South Africa: Evidence from three informal settlements. *International Sociology*, 33(3), 337–356.

Paris, W. M. (2025). *Race, time, and utopia: Critical theory and the process of emancipation*. Oxford University Press.

Parker, I., & Pavón-Cuéllar, D. (2021). *Psychoanalysis and revolution: Critical psychology for liberation movements*. 1968 Press.

Patel, Y. (2020). Meet the artist who painted the George Floyd mural on the separation wall. *Mondoweiss*. Retrieved from https://mondoweiss.net/2020/06/meet-the-a rtist-who-painted-the-george-floyd-mural-on-the-separation-wall.

Pavón-Cuéllar, D. (2017). *Marxism and psychoanalysis: In or against psychology?* Routledge.

Readsura Decolonial Editorial Collective. (2022). Psychology as a site for decolonial analysis. *Journal of Social Issues*, 78(2), 255–277.

Rees, Y. (2021). Thinking capitalism from the bedroom: The politics of location and the uses of (feminist, queer, crip) theory. *Labour History*, 121, 9–31.

Rifkin, M. (2017). *Beyond settler time: Temporal sovereignty and indigenous self-determination*. Duke University Press.

Rose, J. (2011). *Proust among the nations: From Dreyfus to the Middle East*. University of Chicago Press.

Samudzi, Z. (2021). Against genocide: Introduction. *The Funambulist*, 37. Retrieved from https://thefunambulist.net/magazine/against-genocide/against-genocide-introduction.

Seedat, M., & Suffla, S. (2017). Community psychology and its (dis)contents, archival legacies and decolonisation. *South African Journal of Psychology*, 47(4), 421–431.

Sheehi, L. (2022). The ideology of apparitions: Disrupting supremacist temporalities of being (white). *Psychoanalytic Dialogues*, 32(6), 598–609.

Sheehi, L., & Sheehi, S. (2022). *Psychoanalysis under occupation: Practicing resistance in Palestine*. Routledge.

Sheehi, S., & Sheehi, L. (2024). The colonial republic of psychoanalysis: How psychoanalysis polices the psychic sovereignty of "Others". *Psychoanalysis, Culture & Society*, 30(440).

Schmitt, H. J., Young, I. F., Keefer, L. A., Palitsky, R., Stewart, S. A., Goad, A. N., & Sullivan, D. (2021). Time-space distanciation as a decolonizing framework for psychology. *Review of General Psychology*, 25(4), 405–421.

Stevens, G., Duncan, N., & Hook, D. (eds). (2013). *Race, memory and the apartheid archive: Towards a transformative psychosocial praxis.* Springer.

Sultana, F. (2022). The unbearable heaviness of climate coloniality. *Political Geography*, 99, 102638.

Thabolwethu, T. M. & Makama, R. (2025). From colonial time to decolonial temporalities. *British Journal of Social Psychology*, 64(2), e12817.

Traverso, E. (2017). *Left-wing melancholia.* Columbia University Press.

Truscott, R., & Hook, D. (2014). Lessons from the postcolony: Frantz Fanon, psychoanalysis and a psychology of political critique. In P. Nesbitt-Larking, C. Kinnvall, T. Capelos, & H. Dekker (eds), *The Palgrave handbook of global political psychology* (pp. 127–147). Palgrave Macmillan.

White, J. (2024). *In the long run: The future as a political idea.* Profile Books.

Wolpe, H. (1990). *Race, class & the apartheid state.* Africa World Press.

Worby, E., & Ally, S. (2013). The disappointment of nostalgia: Conceptualising cultures of memory in contemporary South Africa. *Social Dynamics*, 39(3), 457–480.

Chapter 6

Not-Yet

Introduction

Ernst Bloch was born in 1885, two years after Marx's death. He is perhaps best remembered today for his philosophy of hope, which, rather audaciously, welded Marxist analysis with the very utopianism that Marx disdained (Greenaway, 2024). Bloch characterised this work as "revolutionary romanticism" (Levitas, 1989). Though not a 'canonical' thinker, academic and political interest in Bloch has been on the rise since his death in 1977. Neither psychology nor psychoanalysis has, however, taken to Bloch's work with much enthusiasm. This is perhaps unsurprising.

Even though scholars like Jameson (1974, p. 121) have characterised Bloch's work as "existential psychology", Bloch himself had little to say on psychology and said nothing at all about liberation psychology. Psychoanalysis, on the other hand, occupies a somewhat different place in Bloch's oeuvre. Bloch (1986 [1954]) held a largely hostile view of psychoanalysis, taking to task many psychoanalytic concepts (e.g. the reality principle, castration anxiety, the unconscious), while remaining bitingly critical of Freud and Jung, the latter of whom Bloch considered a "psychoanalytic fascist" (Levitas, 1989, p. 56). As a Marxist, Bloch (1986 [1954]) felt that psychoanalysis (and presumably also psychology) too often personalised discontent, and thus could only ever offer us a bourgeois picture of the psyche, wherein libidinal wants overshadowed material needs, and the past assumed priority over the future. Additionally, Bloch's thoroughly political conception of hope (which we will look at in more detail below) jars with dominant strands of psychological and psychoanalytic thinking which understand hope as an infantile yearning for what one cannot have, an instrumental/measurable component of goal-setting, or an element of individual 'resilience' (Helman, 2024; Long, 2021).

There are several legitimate reasons as to why anti-capitalist psychological and psychoanalytic practitioners could reject Bloch. For one thing, Bloch's writing is marked by boldfaced Euro- and andro-centric biases. Moreover, there are moments in Bloch's work that lack the clarity needed to articulate

DOI: 10.4324/9781003612728-6

anti-capitalism today. For instance, even though Bloch's anti-Zionism is, at some moments, clear (see Zaretsky, 2024), there are also times in his work where this is less clear. Additionally, we might be resistant to take up Bloch's work due to the hagiographic impulses that so often accompany elevating a single figure, no matter how radical, within political praxis. While I endorse these views, I nonetheless also contend that Bloch's conception of the Not-Yet (a kind of anticipatory disposition that is built and defended with collective struggle) offers a generative and critical lens by which to read and link together the various psycho-political currents that operate in and across anti-capitalist movements. I hope to show in this chapter that the Not-Yet takes us beyond the specific limitations of Bloch's work, and towards an anti-capitalism that is attuned to the patriarchal, imperial, oligarchic, ecocidal, and colonial composition of capital accumulation.

In what follows, I offer a critical appraisal of what Bloch meant by the Not-Yet, particularly as it relates to hope and utopia. I then consider what the Not-Yet might mean for threading together the central concepts explored in this book, namely: political fantasy, the superegoic community, unconsciousness-raising, and memory otherwise. By way of conclusion, I reflect on what the Not-Yet could mean for psychoanalytic liberation psychology praxes concerned with consolidating community-led anti-capitalist movements in and beyond South Africa.

Not-Yet: Anti-Capitalism With and Without Hope

Moving between affective, ideological, and political formations, the Not-Yet represents the anticipated potential for liberation. Bloch (1986 [1954]) outlines two components of the Not-Yet: the Not-Yet-Conscious and the Not-Yet-Become. The Not-Yet-Conscious appears in the fragmented visions of an emancipation to come (Levitas, 1989). It is, as he put it, "a forward dawning, into the New" (Bloch, 1986 [1954], p. 76). It is because the Not-Yet-Conscious is emergent rather than experienced that it calls us to act on its disjointed images of liberation (Jobst, 2021). This brings us to the Not-Yet-Become, the second component of the Not-Yet. The Not-Yet-Become begins the work of building the conditions of emancipation that are alluded to and appear nascently within the Not-Yet-Conscious (Bloch, 1986 [1954]). Although the Not-Yet-Become is enunciated in the present, it is driven by the anticipation of a better future that moves us towards disinvesting psychically in the present (see Everingham, 2016). In this, the present itself emerges as Not-Yet-Become. As a placard from the 2011 Oakland General Strike had it: "The beginning is near" (Holloway, 2019, p. 259).

Within Bloch's conception of the Not-Yet, the Not-Yet-Conscious and the Not-Yet-Become operate in inseparable conjunction. The immaterial imaginative capacities of the Not-Yet-Conscious are crucial for actualising the material dispositions of the Not-Yet-Become (Everingham, 2016). Put differently, if the Not-Yet-Conscious points towards how we might flee from and refuse the onslaughts of capital accumulation (Jobst, 2021), it is the Not-Yet-Become that pushes us to act on these flights and refusals. As Bloch (1986 [1954], p. 127) writes, the "Not-Yet-Conscious as a whole is the psychological representation of the Not-Yet-Become in an age and its world, on the Front of the world". Importantly, where the Not-Yet-Conscious infuses our actions with purpose and desire, the Not-Yet-Become ensures that we do not become immobilised. As Roy (2009, p. 21) asks:

> Are we ready to get off our starting blocks? Are we ready, many millions of us, to rally, not just on the streets, but at work and in schools and in our homes, in every decision we take, and every choice we make? Or not just yet ...?

The Not-Yet is made in contexts of struggle, but it is not the de facto result of struggle. It forms part of the process of struggle. The Not-Yet is embodied in the quotidian of our lives, in the affective encounters of the day-to-day, and in the actions of those who refuse capital's injunctions by doing something else (Holloway, 2019). The Not-Yet attunes us to how the millions of experiments in being otherwise that are taking place all around us are neither disconnected from one another nor are they complete. And that no matter how habitual or powerful our oppression, refusal is always possible (see Everingham, 2016). It is in this regard that Bloch (1986 [1954]) understands the Not-Yet as utopian in its horizons of expectation and perspectives on history (Traverso, 2017). The German word that Bloch used for Not-Yet, *Noch-Nicht*, can indeed be translated as Still-Not, which signifies an asymptotic movement towards utopia (Greenaway, 2024). Utopia, it should be noted, drives but does not altogether swallow the Not-Yet (Jameson, 1974). It orients our desires towards the promises of a completed liberation.

It is difficult to sustain utopia – to nourish the Not-Yet – in the face of political defeat. We should, I believe, push back against those moments in Bloch's work that imply an inevitable or teleological march towards utopia (Jameson, 1974). Writing of the collapse of twentieth-century revolutions, Traverso (2017, p. 119) insists that "utopia does not appear as a 'not yet,' but rather as utopia, a no longer existing place, a destroyed utopia". Utopia is thus not self-sustaining, nor does it inhere within itself a timeless strength. It requires militant defence and facing the material fact that utopia does not exist, or it no longer exists as it once did. Perhaps it never existed. It would, therefore, be inaccurate, Gana (2023) argues, to proclaim that we mourn utopia in moments of defeat. The composition of utopia was always too incomplete for that. Instead, we mourn a particular process of building utopia, and we carry this mourning into how we envision and action utopia in the future. It is a mourning that must not be forgotten or abandoned by the Not-Yet.

Bloch was clear that the Not-Yet is not only utopian. It is also hopeful. He writes, "And so the point is reached where hope itself, this authentic expectant emotion in the forward dream, no longer just appears as merely self-based mental feeling … but in a conscious-known way as utopian function" (Bloch, 1986 [1954], p. 144). Hope is forged in those anticipatory and resistant political actions wherein we find ourselves in unfinished moments of utopia, moments that we may not have hitherto experienced (Jobst, 2021). These moments are intense and enjoyable, and they cannot be entirely predicted. They appear on picket lines, in community gardens, in mutual aid efforts, during strikes, and in the instant of refusal. They allow us "renewed access to some essential source of life" (Jameson, 1974, p. 119).

Hope is, in many respects, to be found in the unfinished nature of our struggles. Just as capitalist domination is not complete, neither is anti-capitalist resistance. As Wolfe (2016, p. 272) notes: "The incompleteness of racial domination is the trace and the achievement of resistance, a space of hope". And as Freire (1997) insists, a minimum of hope is usually required to begin struggling with one another. It is also struggle that sustains hope. We cultivate hope in the solidarity bond, in raging with one another across anti-capitalist struggles (Helman, 2024). It is precisely because hope is structurally limited by capital that "hope is discipline" (Kaba, 2021, p. 26). It must be built and organised if it is to be more convincing and realistic than despair (Williams, 1985). Those who form part of the global food sovereignty movement known as La Via Campesina capture this sentiment with their insistence on "globalising struggle and hope" (Rodríguez & Sosa Varrotti, 2023, p. 575).

We should not, however, make a fetish of hope. History has taught us that "Hope and prediction, though inseparable, are not the same" (Hobsbawm, 2011, p. 72). We may still act to change things even after rational assessment has revealed the hopelessness of our situation. It is sometimes cold analysis, not hope, that is better suited to identifying what and why we must fight. Critical theory does not, after all, need hope (Hook, 2014). It might be courage or a disgust with the state of things – rather than hope – that drives political action (Critchley, 2021). It is also despair over what appears to be an eternally hopeless situation that can motivate some of us to act into this hopelessness, while at the same time rejecting hopeful fantasies that seek to guarantee the outcome of our actions (Žižek, 2017). We should not ignore the potential of a radical hopelessness – "a hopelessness that does not surrender to helplessness" (ka Canham, 2023, p. 4). As Gana (2023, pp. 8–9) writes, "the hopelessness of proactive commitment to a lost cause pales in comparison to the hopelessness of abandoning commitment altogether. It would amount to nothing less than burying the lost cause for the second time". Struggle does not, in every instance, need hope. Many times, we fight the fascist forces of capital because we must. As the late urban historian Mike Davis declared: "Fight with hope, fight without hope, but fight absolutely" (Movaghary-Pour, 2016, paragraph 15).

There exists a dialectical relationship, then, between hope and despair, with the former often revealing itself in the latter (Jameson, 1974). Sultana (2022, p. 2), writing of the climate movement, reflects that a "[s]ense of despair, suffocation, stagnation, abandonment, and regression co-exist with that of revolutionary potentiality, alternative possibilities, collectivizing, world-making, and critical hope". Bloch (1986 [1954]) was clear that the Not-Yet inheres within it a kind of hope that can and will be met with disappointment, but it is a disappointment from which we can learn and that compels us to never accept disappointment as the final or only affective mode of collective struggle (Everingham, 2016).

Hope can serve an affective necessity of survival; one whose operations are not entirely clear to us. Roy (2009, p. xxxvii) recounts the words spoken to her by the widow of Hrant Dink, an Armenian journalist assassinated for speaking out against the Armenian genocide: "We keep hoping. Why do we keep hoping?". Immediate hopelessness can and often is shot through with the hope for something else. This may well be out of the necessity to survive; a will towards sustaining life in conditions of structural death (Helman, 2024; ka Canham, 2023). Something like hope is so often forged out of hopelessness. Dabbagh (2024, paragraph 13) recounts a voice-note received from Marwa, a Palestinian woman describing her community's experience of Zionist-led genocide in Gaza: "I don't know if they are broken or not yet, but what I know is that they try to create hope from nothing, because they don't have another option".

Though the Not-Yet is utopic and hopeful, it is not optimistic. The near certainty of the optimistic position risks complacency – waiting without action and turning away from the material reality to which the Not-Yet is so fiercely attuned. Optimism, as Berlant (2020) observes, can function cruelly. It is, after all, optimism that invests in the upward mobility, bourgeois securities, and equalities that are denied systemically to most people living under capitalism. We wait optimistically for that which capitalism delivers to fewer and fewer people (Helman, 2024). It is with optimism that we adjust to capitalist crisis and move towards tolerating that which is intolerable. Importantly, as Gramsci (1924) argues, rejecting optimism does not mean that we embrace pessimism (an affective position which also breeds passivity). It can also mean embracing the Not-Yet along with the "expectation affects" (Jameson, 1974, p. 127) – like rage, hope, fury, love, bitterness, melancholy, despair, and fear – generated in the fight against capitalist oppression.

Psychoanalytic Liberation Psychology and the Not-Yet

In this section, I take up the Not-Yet as a critical lens – rather than a prophetic declaration (Jameson, 1974) – for reading and making connections between the four concepts used to flesh out psychoanalytic liberation psychology in this book, namely: political fantasy, the superegoic community, unconsciousness-raising, and memory otherwise.

Bloch (1986 [1954]) was critical of fantasy for much the same reason he was critical of psychoanalysis. Fantasy's preoccupation, he argued, lies with the past rather than the emancipatory action that we must take up now if we are to move into a better future. As we saw in Chapter 2, there is certainly a risk that anti-capitalist fantasy becomes mired in static conceptions of the past. And it is not difficult to see how confining the Not-Yet to an irretrievable past risks rendering the Not-Yet irretrievable. However, we also saw in Chapter 2 that fantasy is not only backward-looking. Fantasy can structure people's desire for a world beyond capitalism, animating their anti-capitalist actions. Movements in the south of Johannesburg brought their anti-capitalist fantasies to bear on reality in prefigurative formations (parks and community gardens), radical actions (highway blockades and police confrontations), and formal negotiations (the community-state discussion forum). In attempting to actualise different fantasies in these ways, activists created moments of utopia which encircled the Not-Yet. Here, psychoanalytic liberation psychology does well to attune itself to how struggles move between concrete actions and the fantasies that lie behind these actions, which is to say, the idealism of the Not-Yet-Conscious and the materiality of the Not-Yet-Become. We also saw in Chapter 2 that the fantasy frame does not always hold in the face of capitalism's violent onslaughts. The collapse of the anti-capitalist fantasy frame can give way to grieving the hopes that energised struggles of the past. This, in turn, can inform how people take up, abandon, and reconstitute the Not-Yet in the present. Psychoanalytic liberation psychology must, accordingly, take seriously how such mournful affects surrounding the Not-Yet shape fantasies within anti-capitalist struggle.

Although the scepticism that Bloch (1986 [1954]) held towards fantasy is comparable to how he viewed the superego, he was somewhat less dismissive of the superego, possibly due to the strong influence that the present has on the superegoic command. He argued that the superego tends to appear and disappear in relation to what it demands of the subject and how the subject follows these demands. He also insisted that capitalism's individualising ideologies collapse neat distinctions between id, ego, and superego, writing that: "The ego is its own super-ego and also its own utopic state" (Bloch, 1986 [1954], p. 569). He goes on to state that there is potential strength to be reappropriated from the superego precisely because the superego connects the individual to the social: "the lone individual is ... only a social phenomenon" (Bloch, 1986 [1954], p. 569). Here, I believe that Bloch pushes us to consider the superego in a somewhat more nuanced manner than Freud or Lacan do. There is, indeed, a utopian fantasy of the good life locked into the superegoic command to enjoy capitalist excess, and although this is a fundamentally atomising, divisive – even self-, Other-, and community-ruining –

command, it is nonetheless a command that holds within it the seeds of a genuine hope for something better. As Hobsbawm (1973, p. 166) notes: "the nature of hope is such that there is truth even in the lies of capitalism. The desire for a 'happy end', however commercially exploited, is [our] desire for the good life". The activists in Chapter 4 did not attack those obeying the demands made by the xenophobic superegoic community. Rather, a collectively constituted alternative was offered, one that prioritised the communal modes of living, being, and struggling that are disallowed within the superegoic community. In these alternatives, it became clear that capitalism is a common structural enemy, and it is only by facing this enemy – organising anti-capitalist resistance in relation to it – that the Not-Yet reveals itself. Consequentially, capitalist fantasies of the good life are slowly eroded, and people can assume distance from the superegoic command. The role of psychoanalytic liberation psychology is, here, a practical one: facilitating spaces that reckon with and build solidarity around collective attempts at harnessing the Not-Yet to undermine the grip of the superegoic community.

Bloch (1986 [1954]) devotes much of his energy to a conceptual critique of the unconscious, insisting that repressed material is not as inaccessible or beyond symbolisation as many psychoanalysts believe, and that what is unconscious stands perpetually on the verge of becoming conscious. He also posits that hope guards against the unconscious being stuck in the past by picking up on existing and longed-for traces of the Not-Yet. It seems unlikely, then, that Bloch would have endorsed the unconsciousness-raising process described in Chapter 4. Regardless, as we saw in that chapter, it is with the unconscious that we can reveal and challenge regressive psychic structures operating within anti-capitalist movements, refusing to ensnare subjectivity within these structures (see Parker & Pavón-Cuéllar, 2021). The unconsciousness-raising group recounted in Chapter 4 was demonstrative of how unconsciously held patriarchal positions could be undermined by holding these positions accountable to a consciously professed feminist politics. Although Bloch (1986 [1954]) was adamant that hope and reason nourish one another within the Not-Yet, unconsciousness-raising demonstrates that this may not always be the case; that the rationality of anti-capitalist movements might become unintentionally entwined with the rationality imposed by capital, giving rise to an irrational Not-Yet that is at odds with itself. As Roy (2011, p. 91) writes, we may well find that "hope has little to do with reason". Engaging with the unconscious allowed anti-capitalists working within the psychoanalytic liberation psychology paradigm to use internal tensions to strengthen rather than fracture their movement, and to struggle against that which immanently hinders embracing the Not-Yet.

We should exercise caution when attempting to locate memory in the critical lens offered by the Not-Yet. Bloch's is a future-oriented politics wherein that which is to come is always an open-ended "knowing future capable of being shaped" by the collective (Bloch, 1986 [1954], p. 621). Indeed, for

Bloch, memory is the opposite of hope. It functions as hope's "obverse side, its absolute inversion, in which everything which in reality belongs to the future is attributed to the past, in which time is stood on its head conceptually" (Jameson, 1974, p. 128). Bloch spoke of the *Sperre*, or the block, as a regressive impulse to flee from a seemingly absolute present into a static conception of the past, thereby turning us away from the future-oriented struggles happening around us. While I accept that Bloch may have dismissed Chapter 5's preoccupation with memory, I nonetheless maintain that the Not-Yet forms part of how we construct memory otherwise. And while we might retreat from the urgency of the present into mythic conceptions of the past, community activists in the south of Johannesburg have made clear that the past also contains resources, struggles, lessons, conditions, and affects that bring unfinished conceptions of an emancipated future into the now. These activists re-membered their community struggles through different, sometimes incompatible and contradictory, fragments. As such, the past emerged not as a brute fact, but as a knowingly constructed and multitudinous entity to be taken up, moved through, and activated for different political purposes (e.g. rhetorical, agonistic, consolidatory, adversarial). For psychoanalytic liberation psychology praxis, this means that we need not, in every instance, concern ourselves with the base materiality of history. Rather, what is most salient is how the past is remembered, repressed, reconstituted, and refused by anti-capitalists struggling to return the future to those who have suffered so needlessly under the necropolitical operations of capitalism; those who, in the end, constitute "the class to whom the future belongs" (Marx, 1938, p. 379).

The Not-Yet, I hope to have shown, can assist us in how we perceive and practice psychoanalytic liberation psychology. However, it is also psychoanalytic liberation psychology that stretches the Not-Yet by probing into the various psycho-political phenomena (some of which Bloch was dismissive, such as the unconscious and memory, and some of which he was rather uncritical, like hope) which structure anti-capitalist resistance. The Not-Yet, so conceived, ensures that psychoanalytic liberation psychology moves between whichever forms, approaches, methods, and perspectives are most germane to consolidating anti-capitalism. In this regard, psychoanalytic liberation psychology is, itself, Not-Yet.

At this point, it may be informative to take a step back and look at how the Not-Yet operates at a broader, societal level. In the section that follows, I consider what the Not-Yet has meant, and what it could mean, for practising psychoanalytic liberation psychology in South Africa.

South Africa's Not-Yet

Hope was central to South Africa's nation-building project that began in 1994 during the formal dismantling of the apartheid system. Though fear and anxiety gripped many white nationalists who remained invested in the apartheid regime's racist social ordering, for the vast majority, this was a time marked by hope – the hope of living without segregation and violence, the hope of abolishing state repression, the hopes invested in democracy, the hope of discarding socially poisonous legislation, the hope for a life of dignity and freedom (see Helman, 2024). South Africa's 1994 moment also held out hope for transforming the psy-disciplines (like psychology and psychoanalysis), many of which – especially psychology – had hitherto been central to consolidating apartheid by lending legitimacy to racist labour practices, performing colonial-style cognitive testing, informing racial segregation policy, committing to white supremacist pedagogical practice, and servicing the state's violently oppressive military and police forces (Cooper, 2014; Seedat, 1998). The abolition of apartheid governance, many hoped, presented an opportunity to reconstitute the psy-disciplines so that they might become relevant to the majority and finally break from their shameful past (Bowman et al., 2024).

The social redress that has taken place in South Africa since 1994 should not be ignored. The country boasts among the most progressive constitutions on Earth. Homes, social grants, healthcare, education, and electricity have been provided to millions of South Africans (Levenson, 2022), and progressive elements are operative in the South African state, observed recently in the – albeit uneven (Rawoot, 2023) – Palestinian solidarity efforts undertaken by some state actors. Nonetheless, in South Africa, the ravages of contemporary capitalism[1] have piled onto the legacy of over 400 years of colonial rule. South Africa is, today, one of the most unequal countries in the world (Francis & Webster, 2019). Racialised poverty and spatial segregation remain firmly entrenched, with most of the country's wealth and assets remaining under white ownership. Land in particular continues to function as a commodity (again, mostly white-owned). Such inadequate land reform has meant that colonial and apartheid-era planning has persisted by and large undisturbed (Ngcukaitobi, 2021). Almost a fifth of the country's Black urban population live in shack settlements (Levenson, 2022). Additionally, marginalised majority-Black communities remain chronically under-serviced. Infrastructure in these communities is either crumbling or entirely absent, with hospitals and schools becoming increasingly under-resourced. The country indexes alarmingly high rates of violence, especially gender-based violence (see Boonzaier, 2017; Helman, 2024). South Africa's widespread xenophobia has also been noted for its especially violent character (Dratwa, 2024). The state regularly governs through violent repression, observed, for instance, in the 2012 Marikana Massacre, wherein 34 striking miners were killed by South African police officers (see Long, 2021), the state-led 'siege' of a mine in Stilfontein in 2024, which saw the death of at least 78 artisanal miners (Haffejee, 2025), the violent crackdowns on peaceful protesters and occupants of vacant land (Duncan, 2016), and the assassination of several prominent leaders of Abahlali baseMjondolo, the country's largest shack dwellers' movement (Al-Bulushi, 2024).

The social trajectory of post-1994 South Africa has, in many ways, been mirrored in the disciplinary trajectories of psychology and psychoanalysis (see Hayes, 2008; Suffla et al., 2001). Indeed, it would certainly be a mistake to ignore the politically progressive currents operating within these disciplines today. Both disciplines have, in many respects, sought to align with the country's constitutional commitments to gender and racial equity (Malherbe et al., 2024). Furthermore, the critical traditions of psychological and, albeit to a lesser extent, psychoanalytic praxes – which were instituted in the anti-apartheid community movements (Manganyi, 2019 [1973]; Seedat & Lazarus, 2011) – continue into today, exemplified perhaps most prominently by practitioners embracing the decolonial turn (see e.g. Barnes & Siswana, 2018; Seedat & Suffla, 2017). However, psychology and psychoanalysis in present-day South Africa remain inaccessible to the vast majority (Malherbe et al., 2024). Moreover, most of those trained in these disciplines have been unable to break from Eurocentric, individualising models, contributing little, if anything, to addressing the most pressing socio-political issues facing the country (see Bowman et al., 2024; Hayes, 2008). And although there are undeniably anti-capitalist struggles to which some psychological and psychoanalytic practitioners in South Africa are committed – such as queer and ecological struggles (see Barnes et al., 2022; Pillay et al., 2019) – there are also many practitioners in the country who seek to thwart anti-capitalist psychological work, observed recently in the unsuccessful attempts to prohibit the Psychological Society of South Africa from expressing Palestinian solidarity (Malherbe et al., 2024).

It would appear, then, that within and beyond the psy-disciplines, the hope that characterised South Africa in 1994 has been betrayed in multiple ways. Gobodo-Madikizela (2023, p. 68) reflects that "Not only has this new future of a post-apartheid South Africa not been realised, what remains is a deep disappointment that has collapsed the hope, reaching the depths of feelings of betrayal". Many in South Africa look back at these early moments of hope with intense longing, nostalgia, and even mourning for what could have been. There is, as Chari (2013, p. 149) writes, "a desire for a late-twentieth-century South Africa that could have taken a different turn." Dominant representational apparatuses in the country tend to assess today's situation as fundamentally hopeless. Poor majority-Black communities are frequently portrayed in media, academic, and political narratives through damaged-centred frames that focus on little other than pain, passive victimhood, violence, and brokenness (Boonzaier, 2017). Within these portrayals, marginalised communities in South Africa emerge as doomed to repeat an unreconciled past (Helman, 2024). Much of psychology and psychoanalysis has, unsurprisingly, been part of these narratives, projecting marginalised Black populations in the country as essentially hopeless, often doing so with the assistance of apartheid-era tropes (see Hendricks et al., 2019; Manganyi, 2018).

And yet, South Africa's professional classes are not, thankfully, custodians of the Not-Yet. As has always been the case in South Africa, each day, millions across the country refuse racial capitalism's impositions. They do so with and without hope. South Africa is in many respects a protest nation (Duncan, 2016), one that comprises anti-capitalist struggles for housing, food sovereignty, healthcare, secure employment, land, electricity, water, sanitation, and education. Everywhere there are struggles taking place against gender-based violence, corruption, state abandonment, xenophobia, workplace discrimination, food insecurity, state-directed violence, and austerity. Today's grassroots movements have also continued forging the solidarity relations with Palestine that began in the apartheid-era. This litany of anti-capitalist refusals – usually exhausting and often subject to violent state repression – are willed towards completing the struggles which began in the colonial and apartheid eras. As Bond (2014, p. 122) notes, the contemporary roots of resistance in South Africa

> were seeded not only during the heroic solidarity struggles of the anti-apartheid era, but during the 1990s when the World Bank, IMF and their allies claimed, with the utmost conviction and self-confidence, 'There Is No Alternative' – TINA (the slogan made famous by Margaret Thatcher) – to neoliberal globalisation. South African activists, especially in the Campaign Against Neoliberalism, soon understood the implications of TINA, and learned a rejoinder: 'There Must Be an Alternative' – THEMBA, the Zulu word for 'hope'.

Anti-capitalist struggles in contemporary South Africa feel into, learn from, and take up the anti-colonial commitments of the past. These are psycho-political struggles marked by hope and betrayal, rage and love, solidarity and refusal, mourning and fortitude. They are struggles for the lives that capital extinguishes, abandons, or reduces to mere labour power. They are struggles over the Not-Yet. And they are the struggles which must determine psychoanalytic liberation psychology practice in and beyond South Africa.

Note

1 Hart (2014) has insisted that although it is certainly a capitalist economy that functions in present-day South Africa, it is not especially useful to characterise South African society as *neoliberal,* due in part to state-led developmental initiatives and social grants. The term *neoliberalism,* she argues, also misses the intensely racialised nature of dispossession, expropriation, and exploitation in contemporary South Africa.

References

Al-Bulushi, Y. (2024). *Ruptures in the afterlife of the apartheid city.* Palgrave Macmillan.

Barnes, B., Barnwell, G., & Hendricks, L. (2022). Psychology, environment and climate change: Foregrounding justice (part one). *Psychology in Society,* 63, 1–5.

Barnes, B., & Siswana, A. (2018). Psychology and decolonisation: Introduction to the special issue. *South African Journal of Psychology,* 48(3), 297–298.

Berlant, L. (2020). *Cruel optimism.* Duke University Press.

Bloch, E. (1986 [1954]). *The principle of hope.* MIT Press.

Bond, P. (2014). *Elite transition: From apartheid to neoliberalism in South Africa.* Pluto.

Boonzaier, F. (2017). The life and death of Anene Booysen: Colonial discourse, gender-based violence and media representations. *South African Journal of Psychology,* 47(4), 470–481.

Bowman, B., Malherbe, N., & Suffla, S. (2024). Three decades of psychology in South Africa: Legacies of hope and fault lines of the future. *South African Journal of Psychology,* 54(4), 423–436.

Chari, S. (2013). Detritus in Durban: Polluted environs and the biopolitics of refusal. In L. A. Stoler (ed.), *Imperial debris: On ruins and ruination* (pp. 131–161). Duke University Press.

Cooper, S. (2014). A synopsis of South African psychology from apartheid to democracy. *American Psychologist,* 68, 837–847.

Critchley, S. (2021). *Bald: 35 philosophical short cuts.* Yale University Press.

Dabbagh, S. (2024). Hope from nothing. *London Review of Books Blog.* Retrieved from www.lrb.co.uk/blog/2024/july/hope-from-nothing.

Dratwa, B. (2024). Xenophobia: A pervasive crisis in post-apartheid South Africa. *Georgetown Journal of International Affairs.* Retrieved from https://gjia.georgetown.edu/2024/05/26/xenophobia-a-pervasive-crisis-in-post-apartheid-south-africa.

Duncan, J. (2016). *Protest nation: The right to protest in South Africa.* University of KwaZulu-Natal Press.

Everingham, P. (2016). Hopeful possibilities in spaces of 'the-not-yet-become': Relational encounters in volunteer tourism. *Tourism Geographies,* 18(5), 520–538.

Francis, D., & Webster, E. (2019). Poverty and inequality in South Africa: Critical reflections. *Development Southern Africa,* 36(6), 788–802.

Freire, P. (1997). *Pedagogy of hope.* Continuum.

Gana, N. (2023). *Melancholy acts: Defeat and cultural critique in the Arab world.* Fordham University Press.

Gramsci, A. (1924). Against pessimism. *L'Ordine Nuovo: Rassegna Settimanale di Cultura Socialista,* 15, 1921–1926.

Greenaway, J. (2024). *A primer on utopian philosophy: An introduction to the work of Ernst Bloch.* Zero Books.

Gobodo-Madikizela, P. (2023). The afterlife of apartheid: a triadic temporality of trauma. *Social Dynamics,* 49(1), 67–86.

Haffejee, I. (2025). "The smell of death was everywhere" – Stilfontein mine rescue ends. *GroundUp.* Retrieved from https://groundup.org.za/article/the-smell-of-death-was-everywhere-stilfontein-mine-rescue-ends.

Hart, G. (2014). *Rethinking the South African crisis: Nationalism, populism, hegemony.* University of Georgia Press.

Hayes, G. (2008). Psychoanalysis in the shadow of post-apartheid reconstruction. *Theory & Psychology*, 18(2), 209–222.

Helman, R. (2024). Hope in the wake of rape: Mourning, rage and refusal in womxn's accounts of sexual violation. *Annual Review of Critical Psychology*, 18, 1105–1127.

Hendricks, L., Kramer, S., & Ratele, K. (2019). Research shouldn't be a dirty thought, but race is a problematic construct. *South African Journal of Psychology*, 49(3), 308–311.

Hobsbawm, E. (1973). *Revolutionaries*. Abacus.

Hobsbawm, E. (2011). *On history*. Hachette.

Holloway, J. (2019). *We are the crisis of capital: A John Holloway reader*. PM Press.

Hook, D. (2014). Antagonism, social critique and the "violent reverie". *Psychology in Society*, 46, 21–34.

Jameson, F. (1974). *Marxism and form: Twentieth-century dialectical theories of literature*. Princeton University Press.

Jobst, S. (2021). The Principle of Hope: Bloch's contribution to the praxiological understanding of education. *Conflict & Communication*, 20(2), 1–8.

ka Canham, H. (2023). *Riotous deathscapes*. Duke University Press.

Kaba, M. (2021). *We do this 'til we free us: Abolitionist organizing and transforming justice*. Haymarket Books.

Levenson, Z. (2022). *Delivery as dispossession: Land occupation and eviction in the postapartheid city*. Oxford University Press.

Levitas, R. (1989). Marxism, romanticism and utopia: Ernst Bloch and William Morris. *Radical Philosophy*, 51, 27–36.

Long, W. (2021). *Nation on the couch: Inside South Africa's mind*. Melinda Ferguson Books.

Malherbe, N., Suffla, S., Bowman, B., Cooper, S., Foxcroft, C., Mashego, T., … & Watts, A. (2024). Looking backwards, looking forwards: Collective and critical conversations on psychology in South Africa. *South African Journal of Psychology*, 54(4), 437–450.

Manganyi, N. C. (2019 [1973]). *Being-black-in-the-world*. Wits University Press.

Manganyi, N. C. (2018). Making strange: Race science and ethnopsychiatric discourse. *Psychology in Society*, 57, 4–23.

Marx, K. (1938). A workers' inquiry. *New International*, 4(12), 379–381.

Movaghary-Pour, P. (2016). Interview: "Fight with hope, fight without hope, but fight absolutely" with Mike Davis. *LSE Blog*, Retrieved from https://blogs.lse.ac.uk/researchingsociology/2016/03/01/fight-with-hope-fight-without-hope-but-fight-absolutely-an-interview-with-mike-davis/.

Ngcukaitobi, T. (2021). *Land matters: South Africa's failed land reforms and the road ahead*. Random House.

Parker, I., & Pavón-Cuéllar, D. (2021). *Psychoanalysis and revolution: Critical psychology for liberation movements*. 1968 Press.

Pillay, S. R., Nel, J. A., McLachlan, C., & Victor, C. J. (2019). Queering the history of South African psychology: From apartheid to LGBTI+ affirmative practices. *American Psychologist*, 74(8), 954–966.

Rawoot, I. (2023). Solidarity means more than words. *Africa is a Country*. Retrieved from https://africasacountry.com/2023/11/solidarity-means-more-than-words.

Rodríguez, F., & Sosa Varrotti, A. P. (2023). Thirty years of sowing hope to globalise the struggle: Women and youth of La Via Campesina in the construction of food sovereignty–a conversation. *The Journal of Peasant Studies*, 50(2), 559–577.

Roy, A. (2009). *Listening to grasshoppers: Field notes on democracy.* Penguin.

Seedat, M. (1998). A characterisation of South African psychology (1948–1988): The impact of exclusionary ideology. *South African Journal of Psychology,* 28(2), 74–84.

Seedat, M., & Lazarus, S. (2011). Community psychology in South Africa: Origins, developments, and manifestations. *Journal of Community Psychology,* 39(3), 241–257.

Seedat, M., & Suffla, S. (2017). Community psychology and its (dis)contents, archival legacies and decolonisation. *South African Journal of Psychology,* 47(4), 421–431.

Suffla, S., Stevens, G., & Seedat, M. (2001). Mirror reflections: The evolution of organised psychology in South Africa. In N. Duncan, A. van Niekerk, C. de la Rey, & M. Seedat (eds), *Race, racism, knowledge production and psychology in South Africa* (pp. 27–36). Nova Science Publishers.

Sultana, F. (2022). The unbearable heaviness of climate coloniality. *Political Geography,* 99, 102638.

Traverso, E. (2017). *Left-wing melancholia.* Columbia University Press.

Williams, R. (1985). *Towards 2000.* Pelican Books.

Wolfe, P. (2016). *Traces of history: Elementary structures of race.* Verso.

Zaretsky, E. (2024). Israel and the crisis in Judaism. *London Review of Books Blog.* Retrieved from https://www.lrb.co.uk/blog/2024/february/israel-and-the-crisis-in-judaism.

Žižek, S. (2017). *The courage of hopelessness: Chronicles of a year of acting dangerously.* Penguin.

Index

Adams, G. 106, 111–112
Afuape, Taiwo 14
A. K. Rice Institute 85–86
Alexander, N. 111
Ali, N. B. 83
Amin, S. 5
Anderson, P. 6
antagonism 46
anti-capitalism: formation of 9; non-capitalism vs 7–8; overview 5–9; political use-value of 8–9; as psychological undertaking 3; worldview of 24
anti-capitalist activism 109
anti-capitalist movements 47–52, 106
anti-capitalist resistance 5–6
anti-capitalist revolutions 5
anti-colonial resistance 43
anti-xenophobic interventions 70–71
Apartheid Archive Project 108
Argentina, National Front Against Poverty 5

Behagel, J. H. 38
Benjamin, W. 105, 106
Berlant, L. 121
Berlin Poliklinik 14
Berlin Psychoanalytic Institute 14
Bernays, E. 11–12
Bhabha, H. 104
Biko, S. 81–82
Bion, W. R. 85
Black Consciousness 81–82
Bloch, E. 7; conception of Not-Yet 118; as critical of fantasy 122; as a Marxist 117; on Not-Yet-Conscious 119; on psychoanalysis 117; on the unconscious 123
Bond, P. 5, 127

Brown, W. 102
Byrne, K. 46

capital: psychic investment in 40–41; unconscious attachments to 40–41
capital accumulation 6, 11–12, 67, 103
capitalism: damages in fight against 49; definition of 6; as institutionalised social order 6–7; Marx on 72; social order 65; stability of 6; superegoic community and 63–65
capitalist accumulation 63, 69, 73, 100–101
capitalist fantasies 39–43
capitalist mode of production 18
capitalist oppression 19–20
Caputo, A. 61
Carter, C. J. 12, 15
Chamberlain, M. 12
Chari, S. 126
Chavis, D. M. 58
collective power 25
colonial capitalism: psychoanalysis under 11; psychoanalytic institutions' collusion with 12–13
colonial fantasies 42–43
community: bound up with positivism 57; definition of 57–58; determining good from bad 57–58; dynamic qualities of 61–62; Lacanian superego and 65; in political terms 66–68; psychoanalytic formulation of 62; static conceptions of 72; static notions of 59
community of things 72–73
community psychologists: margin-alisation of psychoanalysis within 60–61; understandings of community 58–59

For Product Safety Concerns and Information please contact our EU
representative GPSR@taylorandfrancis.com
Taylor & Francis Verlag GmbH, Kaufingerstraße 24, 80331 München, Germany

www.ingramcontent.com/pod-product-compliance
Lightning Source LLC
Chambersburg PA
CBHW050615280326
41932CB00016B/3050